FLYING GEESE

NEW QUILTS FROM AN OLD FAVORITE

AQS Publishing

edited by LINDA BAXTER LASCO

IN APPRECIATION

The National Quilt Museum thanks the
2017 sponsors of New Quilts from an Old Favorite: Flying Geese.

JANOME

moda

Located in Paducah, Kentucky, the American Quilter's Society (AQS) is dedicated to promoting the accomplishments of today's quilters. Through its publications and events, AQS strives to honor today's quiltmakers and their work and to inspire future creativity and innovation in quiltmaking.

Senior Editor: Linda Baxter Lasco
Copy Editor: Chrystal Abhalter
Graphic Design: Lynda Smith
Cover Design: Michael Buckingham
Quilt Photography: Charles R. Lynch

Additional copies of this book may be ordered from the American Quilter's Society, PO Box 3290, Paducah, KY 42002-3290, or online at www.AmericanQuilter.com.
Text © 2017, American Quilter's Society
Artwork © 2017, American Quilter's Society

American Quilter's Society
P.O. Box 3290 • Paducah, KY 42002-3290
Fax 270-898-1173 • e-mail: orders@AQSquilt.com

Library of Congress Cataloging-in-Publication Data

Cover quilt: MIGRATION PATTERNS by Susan Mogan. Full quilt page 10.
Title page quilt: GLAD PLAID GOOSE DANCE by Ann L. Petersen. Full quilt page 74.
Quilt detail to left: DESTINATION UNKNOWN by Mary Kay Davis. Full quilt page 46.

DEDICATION

This book commemorates the 2017 New Quilts from an Old Favorite:
Flying Geese contest, exhibit, and quilters.

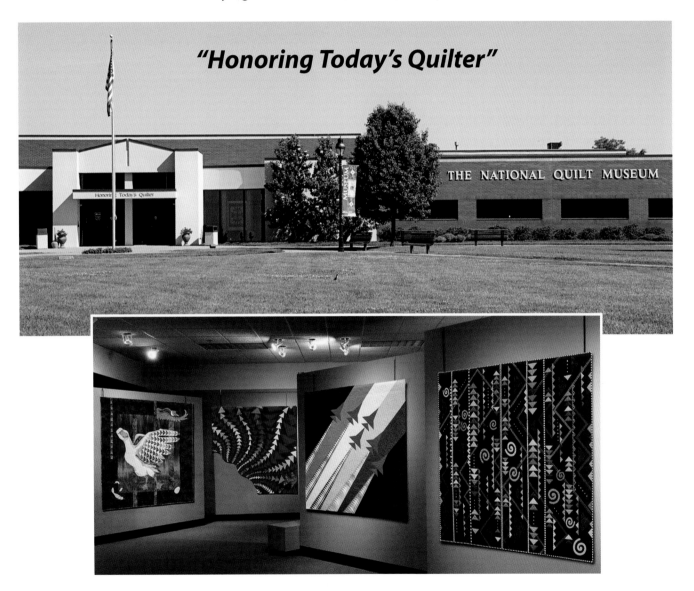

Dedicated to the quilters who celebrate the craft of quilting using a
traditional block pattern to create an innovative work of art.

CONTENTS

Preface..5

The Contest 6

The Flying Geese Block 7

First Place:

    Susan Mogan, MIGRATION PATTERNS 10

Second Place:

    Robin Gausebeck, SATURDAY NIGHT AT THE
        HONK-Y TONK SALOON 16

Third Place:

    Colleen Eskridge & Judy Stokes,
        SOARING TO NEW HEIGHTS 20

Fourth Place:

    Leslie Johnson, I DON'T KNOW IF I'M COMING OR GOING. . 26

Fifth Place:

    Patricia Hobbs, JACOB'S PLUMAGE 32

Finalists:

    Jean Brueggenjohann, ON THE WINGS OF ETERNITY 36

    Tere D'Amato, WELKOM NEDERLAND 42

    Mary Kay Davis, DESTINATION UNKNOWN 46

    Gail Garber & Kris Vierra, CELEBRATION 52

    Julia Graber, TWIRLY BIRDS 56

    Charlene Hearst, POURSUITE D'OIE SAUVAGE À PARIS......... 60
        (WILD GOOSE CHASE IN PARIS)

    Anita Karban-Neef, FLY AWAY HOME 64

    Chris Lynn Kirsch, SILLY GOOSE 68

    Ann L. Petersen, GLAD PLAID GOOSE DANCE 74

    Katie Pidgeon, LUCY GOOSY @ THE IMPROV 78

    Alicia Sterna, CHILLY GOOSE, NO FEATHERS 82

    Sue Turnquist, FARM ALARM 86

    Jane Zillmer, MOONLIGHT MIGRATION 90

The National Quilt Museum....................... 94

PREFACE

The National Quilt Museum celebrates its 26th year of service to the quilting community in 2017. Since the museum's opening in 1991, millions of people from the 50 states and over 60 foreign countries have learned about the extraordinary artwork created by quilters through the efforts of the museum.

Annually, the museum sponsors a contest based on a traditional quilt pattern. The challenge to quiltmakers stems from the contest name—New Quilts from an Old Favorite. This year's theme is the Flying Geese block. An exhibit of contest winners and finalists is held each year at the museum.

This book is a collection of the most innovative quilts entered in the contest. Inside you will meet the quilters, discover their inspiration, and follow their techniques. You will see the color, the creativity, and the craft of a widely diverse group.

An introduction to the museum and its mission are included in the book. You will learn about the continued efforts of the museum to advance quilting through exhibits, education, and advocacy. See http://quiltmuseum.org/education/contests/new-quilts-old-favorites/ for information about the travel schedule for this year's exhibit.

Our hope is that the quilts will provide motivation for all quilters to consider their own interpretation of a traditional block to create a new quilt from an old favorite.

Judy Schwender
Curator of Collections/Registrar
The National Quilt Museum

THE CONTEST

The role of a museum is to preserve the past, but the role extends to connect the past to the present and to the future. The National Quilt Museum fulfills that role through an annual contest and exhibit called New Quilts from an Old Favorite. This contest is to acknowledge our quiltmaking heritage and to recognize innovation, creativity, and excellence. New Quilts from an Old Favorite challenges today's quiltmakers to create a quilt though the interpretation of a single traditional quilt block.

The contest requires the quilts to be a recognizable variation of the selected traditional block. The quilt must measure between 50" and 80" per side. Each entry must be quilted. Only designers and quilters can enter their original work; no kits are accepted. The quilt must be completed within two years of the entry due date.

(See http://quiltmuseum.org/education/contests/new-quilts-old-favorites/) for details.

For the preliminary judgment, quiltmakers send in two photographs of their quilts—one showing the full quilt and one close-up providing the jurors an opportunity to view the details of the quilt. Three jurors study these photo images considering technique, artistry, and interpretation of the theme block to select 18 finalists. The selected quilts are sent to the museum. A different panel of three judges carefully evaluates the quilts focusing on design, innovation, theme, and workmanship. After the evaluations are complete, the judges confer and select the 1st through 5th place winners.

Our New Quilts from an Old Favorite exhibit opens at The National Quilt Museum in Paducah, Kentucky, each spring, featuring the quilts of both winners and finalists. After the museum exhibit closes, the quilts tour for two years. Across the nation quilt lovers are able to view these innovative works of art.

Accompanying the New Quilts from an Old Favorite contest and exhibit is a book of the same name. Produced by the American Quilter's Society and AQS Publishing, it features full-color photos of the award-winning quilts and finalists, biographical information about each quilter, the inspiration for the design, and the use of techniques in the creation of the quilt. This provides an inside look at how these quilts are created and a glimpse into the artistic mindset of today's quilters.

Previous theme blocks have been Double Wedding Ring, Log Cabin, Ohio Star, Mariner's Compass, Pineapple, Kaleidoscope, Storm at Sea, Bear's Paw, Tumbling Block, Feathered Star, Monkey Wrench, Seven Sisters, Dresden Plate, Rose of Sharon, Sawtooth, Burgoyne Surrounded, Sunflower, Orange Peel, Baskets, Jacob's Ladder, Carolina Lily, Nine Patch, and New York Beauty. Blocks selected for future contests are the Bow Tie (2018) and Oak Leaf & Reel (2019).

THE FLYING GEESE BLOCK

The most interesting aspect of the Flying Geese block is its simplicity:

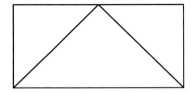

See the *Encyclopedia of Pieced Quilt Patterns* (American Quilter's Society) by Barbara Brackman, No. 2902 to No. 2913 .

This unit can be used as the sole element in a quilt. It can be used for sashing, for borders, or as part of a block, either pieced or with appliqué. It's like the Nine-Patch and Four-Patch blocks; they are the amino acids of quilting—essential to its existence.

An advanced search of Flying Geese quilts on the Quilt Index (www.quiltindex.org) produced 217 results. Some were excluded because the unit used was not the Flying Geese block as seen above. One quilt was of Log Cabin blocks in a Flying Geese set. Also excluded were quilts with blocks made up of half-square triangles, which produces something of a faux Flying Geese unit. The resulting 185 quilts could be sorted into six groups:

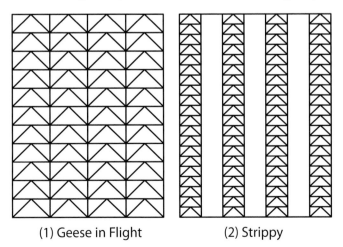

(1) Geese in Flight   (2) Strippy

(3) Flying Geese units as the only element (including the Wild Goose Chase block and strippy quilts)

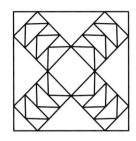

(4) Flying Geese units as an element in the sashing, borders, or as part of a pieced block

(5) Doll quilts (Two were composed of Flying Geese units.)

(6) Crib quilts (Only one was made of Flying Geese units.)

In the sampling, Flying Geese units were used as an element most often from 1850 to 1925 with 1900 to 1925 as the period of most use. The Geese in Flight quilt was most often found from 1850 to 1875. Flying Geese units as the only element were mostly found from 1825 to 1875; there was a slight resurgence in the 1900 to 1925 time frame. This analysis coincides with the first blossoming of quilting in the general American population, the mid-nineteenth century and the period surrounding the First World War, right before the Depression.

Today's quiltmakers can create really appealing scrappy quilts by using Flying Geese units made from the light and dark fabrics in their stash. Based on the sampling from the Quilt Index, the quiltmakers from more than 100 years ago did the same thing. These units allow quilters to indulge their love of printed fabrics, and that love has been shared by quiltmakers throughout the centuries.

Judy Schwender
Curator, The National Quilt Museum
January 12, 2017

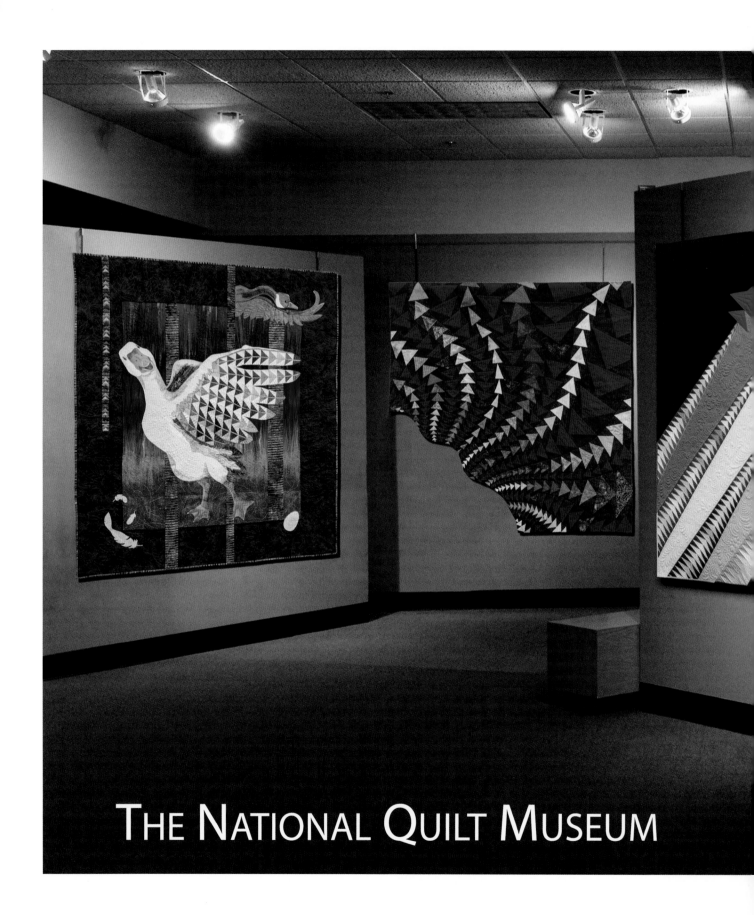

THE NATIONAL QUILT MUSEUM

The National Quilt Museum
215 Jefferson Street • Paducah • Kentucky 42001 • www.quiltmuseum.org • (270) 442-8856

First Place

SUSAN MOGAN

Mobile, Alabama

Meet Susan

Photo by JCPenney Portraits

My quilting journey began in 2005, after wandering into a fabric store and seeing bright and colorful quilts displayed on the wall. Up until that time, I had never liked quilts because all the ones I had seen were in dull or faded colors, and I am a color fanatic. I took my first quilting class shortly before moving to Paducah, Kentucky, in 2006. Being new to quilting, it took me a few years before I joined the local guild there, where I met a wonderful group of friends and mentors. I joke to people that joining a quilt guild is like belonging to the mob: once you're in you can never get out! And of course Paducah is Quilt City USA, so what better place to begin?

Living in Paducah meant that I could visit The National Quilt Museum whenever I wanted, which was an incredible source of inspiration and learning for me. My dream was to someday have one of my quilts hanging there. That dream was realized in 2014, when I was a finalist in the New Quilts from an Old Favorite: Nine Patch contest. I had moved to Mobile by that time, but was able to travel to see the quilt hanging there in person—an unbelievable thrill. You can imagine how ecstatic I was upon learning my quilt MIGRATION PATTERNS had won first place in this year's contest!

I am an art quilter. All of the quilts I make are designed strictly as creative expressions, and almost every quilt I have ever made is an original design. I especially love the New Quilts from an Old Favorite contest because I have always been very interested in seeing how different people interpret the same concept. I love seeing the range of literal representation to extreme abstraction that results from this type of contest, and I find that this always helps me expand my own ways of approaching a subject. When I begin to design a new quilt, the problem for me is not coming up with an idea, it is that I have too many ideas and narrowing it down to something manageable in one quilt is very difficult. Being unable to decide on a starting point can leave me stymied for weeks. The NQOF contest provides a starting point for a design, and imposes just the right combination of restriction and freedom to make for a great experience.

I am fortunate to belong to both a great guild in Mobile and a very active group of art quilters who inspire me and keep me excited about my own creative journey. We explore a wide variety of techniques and materials and do a lot of collaborative group projects, which has resulted in numerous exhibits of our work around Mobile. I am also blessed to have a husband who lets me buy as much fabric as I want, three wonderful grown children, and sisters and friends to support me, inspire me, and keep me from going too far off on tangents to ever get anything actually accomplished. Quilting really is a wonderful world full of great, caring people, and I am thrilled to be a part of it.

Inspiration

Growing up in Ohio, seeing geese flying south for the winter was an annual event. There was always something a little melancholy and yet stirring about it, as it marked the passing of time and coming of winter while also hinting at exotic destinations and adventures. I always felt a sense of wanderlust seeing their V formations overhead, disappearing into the distance.

When I first saw the theme for this year's contest, I wasn't sure I would participate because I just couldn't come up with a design I thought was both interesting and original. I kept trying to create something really funky from the traditional Flying Geese block, but in my head all I kept seeing were Vs of migrating geese crisscrossing each other across the sky, and the intriguing new patterns that were created by this, so I finally decided to go with that as my overall design.

I love lots of color, so I chose bright solids and used them in large-scale triangles to create a bold color impact. I placed the large triangles to imitate the way the geese stagger themselves in flight, and used the warm and cool colors to suggest how the geese migrate based on changing temperatures. Smaller sets of both staggered and straight-line triangles were used to lead the eye through the quilt and to add visual interest through varying scale, with neutral grays and whites as counterpoints to the color. The large gray and red V's suggest the different flocks as their flight patterns overlap each other in the sky.

This design is only the second modern quilt I have done (the first was Modern Nine Patch for the 2014 NQOF contest). I usually tend toward complex, busy designs, so creating a minimalistic design was outside my comfort zone. I had to constantly remind myself to not start adding a lot of extra elements as I worked (as you will see in the later photos). I did add some additional visual interest through the quilting patterns, but again had to remind myself to keep the quilting to the same clean feel and larger scale as the overall quilt design.

I learned that a successful minimalistic design is harder to do than it sounds, as each element carries more responsibility for the total effect than in a more complex design. I kept trying to fill in both the areas of negative space and the large triangles with more detail. While I did succumb to adding some stripes to the large colored triangles, I managed to not go overboard. The quilt top underwent a somewhat substantial change as I worked, which is not uncommon for me. I find the design that I visualize in my head usually needs some tweaking when I actually see it made up in color and to scale.

What I love about this quilt is the impact of the color. The simplicity of the design allows the colors to really stand out, and the size of each piece intensifies this. The contrast of the bright white with the colors is fresh and energizing, and the changing directions of the triangles give the quilt motion and energy. I may actually explore this concept of minimalism in future quilts, as I found it forced me to think a little differently.

Technique and Construction

Once I finally decided on my overall concept of overlapping Vs and triangles, I did a few small, very rough sketches to audition different compositions and layouts. I then chose the one I thought had the most visual interest and balance and did a more detailed sketch of it, although, as you can see, the sketch is still a little rough.

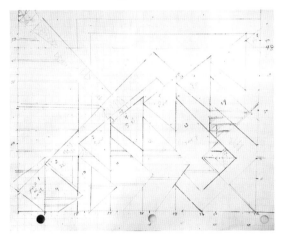

Since I had never done such a minimalistic design before, I made a small (roughly 11" x 16") mock-up of the basic design. I wanted just to see how the large blocks of color and the gray contrast would read and whether the design was, in fact, too simple.

The colors and shapes created what I thought was a successful design, so my next step was to enlarge it to the final size. Since both my original drawing and my mock-up were in rough form, I had to draw the enlarged pattern by hand using some very long rulers and protractors, drawing some angles by eye until I thought I had it right. Maybe one of these days I'll learn how to do computer drafting or design and this process will become much easier, but I'm usually too impatient to get started on the quilt to spend the time learning how to do that.

Once the full-size pattern was drawn, I began the piecing. MIGRATION PATTERNS is all pieced, with the exception of the machine-appliquéd circles. Here the original top is completed, although not entirely sewn together.

It wasn't wowing me, so I started playing with what I could add to make it more visually exciting. Remember how I said it was difficult not to start adding a lot more design elements? This shows my attempt to include the stripes that were part of the original mock-up into the larger top.

I sent this photo to my support people, and while the verdict was mixed on whether to include the stripes or not, my sister commented that she did not like the stripes in the large gray triangle on the left of the quilt.

This made me take a hard look to see if I agreed. I realized I didn't love that part either, so I tore it out and put a large gray solid triangle there instead. That was when I realized that the real problem was not the stripes—it was the gray triangle itself. So I tore out that entire section of the top and started over.

This is a common occurrence with me when designing a quilt, as I often find that a design looks different made-up than it does in my head. Thank goodness for seam rippers! I began trying out different colors and designs to replace it, along with the idea of adding wonky multicolored stripes in different areas.

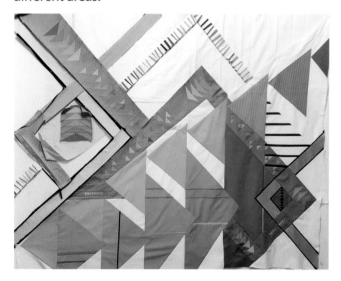

While I loved the idea of the wonky stripes in the quilt, I felt that all of those small pieces diluted the impact of the large blocks of solid color and detracted from the design. I tried some changes, but again there was something bothering me about it; there just wasn't enough energy. Then, eureka! I had the inspiration to change the large V coming in from the left from gray to red and that made all the difference in the world to the overall impact. It added so much energy to the quilt and pulled the red from the far right across the surface of the quilt, tying everything together.

I did all of the quilting on MIGRATION PATTERNS with my walking foot. While I know how to do free-motion quilting, I felt that the quilting should be more angular and geometric to match the feel of the design. However, I did plan in some quilted circles inside the large colored triangles just for some movement and to counterbalance all the straight lines. A friend suggested I appliqué colored circles inside the quilting shapes. While I decided against that, once again the comment made me take another look at the quilt and start playing with placing the circles in other areas. Even though the quilt was almost completely quilted, I ended up loving the energy and slight sense of whimsy the circles added to the quilt when placed in the negative space between the triangles. So I appliquéd them onto the top and balanced the blue and green ones with a few warm-colored ones at the top.

As you can see, even though I had done a mock-up before starting, the quilt design still evolved quite a bit over the course of the construction. I believe it's important to work visually, to let your quilt speak to you about what it needs, and to be willing to make changes or even start over if that's what it takes to make it the best it can be.

I am so grateful for having people around me who are not afraid to give me constructive criticism and honest feedback, which is not an easy thing to do, as well as throw out additional ideas for consideration. One of the best things about quilting is making new relationships. Sharing ideas, problems, frustrations, successes, and finally the finished quilt with friends and family makes it so much more enjoyable than just doing something alone!

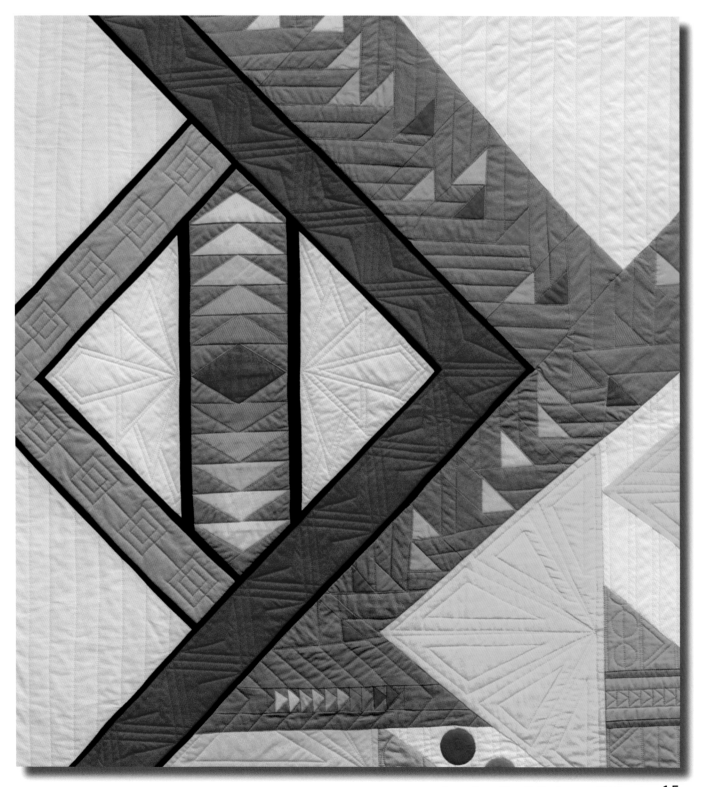

SATURDAY NIGHT AT THE HONK-Y TONK SALOON 65" x 59"

Second Place
ROBIN GAUSEBECK
Rockford, Illinois

Meet Robin

Photo by Steven R. Gausebeck

New Quilts from an Old Favorite is a theme that has fascinated me since my first entry of a Sawtooth quilt in the 2008 contest. There is no history of quilting in my family and I did not grow up with quilts in my home. When I started quilting about eleven years ago, I managed to entirely skip the traditional and dove headlong into contemporary quilting. Designing quilts for NQOF is the one way I have to keep my work grounded in tradition while staying true to my artistic aesthetic.

Quilting became a part of my life after early retirement, when I made a very basic quilt to fill an empty wall in my stairwell. I had not taken any lessons, so that first quilt, while very attractive, always makes me cringe at all the novice mistakes I made. Something about working with color and fabric really resonated with me and a quilter was born. Since then, I have taken as many quilting classes as I can. My guild, Sinnissippi Quilters of Rockford, Illinois, brings in excellent speakers each year and I have traveled to Paducah and Houston each

year to take advantage of the wonderful teachers that those shows highlight. Perhaps the most fun of all is taking a multi-day workshop at The National Quilt Museum.

While I have made large wedding quilts for my children and a couple of bed-size quilts for our home, I usually work either in miniature or wall-size. It seems to be easier for me to express my ideas on a more limited canvas. I have many more ideas than will ever be turned into quilts, and most of the time those ideas begin with a quilt title. Wordplay, puns, and puzzles are nearly as much fun for me as quilting, and I like my quilt titles to express some quirkiness. That seems backwards but I appear to be much more comfortable with words than with visual images, something that I know I should work to change.

This black and colorful quilt with an abundance of shapes made me think of a rip-roaring, raucous Saturday night at an old-time quintessential American saloon of the 1800s—

perhaps a place where a bunch of crazy geese could go for a "honking" good time (add groan here).

These days, my three young grandchildren occupy a lot of my time and energy. Charlotte, the oldest at seven, was the inspiration for my winning NQOF Nine Patch quilt a couple of years ago, and it will be hers when she's old enough to care for it properly. She has learned to sew on my BERNINA and is looking forward to attending quilt camp at The National Quilt Museum this summer. Five-year-old Jeffrey just designed and made his first "quilt" and shows great promise as well.

My husband, Steve, remains my greatest supporter, willing to offer advice when asked and lending a critical eye to my designs. Through my quilting, he has gotten to know many people in the quilting world and loves to bring friends to The National Quilt Museum where he is a knowledgeable guide for whatever exhibit is on display.

Inspiration and Design

I must sound like a broken record sometimes—(1) get a great idea for NQOF; (2) design the quilt top; (3) construct the quilt top; (4) begin quilting; (5) after months of work, decide that I don't like it at all and start over again from scratch. SATURDAY NIGHT AT THE HONK-Y TONK SALOON was no different. The first top was completed in October 2015 but the quilting was a disaster. That quilt will never see the light of day. HONK-Y TONK was begun a few short months before the deadline and, after many long days at the machine, finished with time to spare.

The basic inspiration came when I did something for the very first time and purchased strips of fabrics that caught my eye—a Timeless Treasures textured blender in a variety of colors. The 2½" strips seemed just big enough to turn into Flying Geese in both 3" and 4" widths

At this point, it would be wonderful if I could offer some interesting and helpful insights into my design process that could be useful to other quilters. I'm almost embarrassed to say that all I did was take

some graph paper, draw a rectangle, sketch in columns that were either 3" or 4" wide, and populate the columns with groups of Flying Geese.

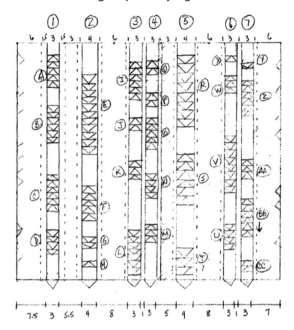

I played around a little until the arrangement was pleasing to my eye and added some narrow black-and-white striped sections for visual interest.

This is the point at which my nerdiness kicked in. In the sketch, it is clear that I have labeled all the geese units with a letter designation. I needed a way to keep track of the 29 geese I had to print from Electric Quilt 7® software for my foundation paper piecing and what the specifics of each unit were in both size and number. I needed to be organized. This is what Excel spreadsheets are for.

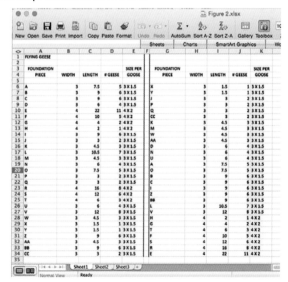

Once I had laid out the details of each unit on the spreadsheet, I could reorder the units to make printing and construction efficient. After all, this was September and the contest deadline was less than two months away!

After each of the long strips was stitched, including joining the geese with the black pieces, the process became a little trickier. One of the most enjoyable parts of designing a quilt for NQOF is imagining how many different ways the theme block can be incorporated into the quilt. Having recently learned how to make Prairie Points, I used some of these along the left and right edges to help "enclose" the body of the quilt. Additional strings of black-and-white geese were fused along seamlines to break up larger expanses of black. The spirals, which have no symbolic relation to geese, were thrown in for no reason except for the fun of it.

Finally, I decided to add long lines of decorative quilting to run parallel to some of the angles formed by the geese. I used a variety of narrow fill designs and did that part of the quilting with brightly colored thread. I inserted additional geese by quilting gridded triangles with variegated thread.

Technique
The process of constructing Flying Geese using foundation paper piecing produces sharp points and consistently sized blocks with a great deal of accuracy. I do not intend to have a tutorial on that here. I'm including these two units so that anyone who does not have EQ7 can use what I have already done. Flying Geese of any dimension can easily be drafted by hand as well, using these templates as a guide.

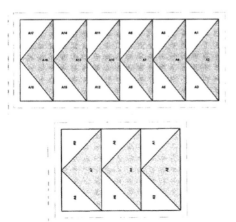

Instead, I want to briefly discuss the design maxim "less is more." Once I had finalized the overall design, my imagination began to work in overdrive. What else fun and funky could I add to this quilt to increase the feeling of whimsicality and craziness? In my sketch, there are some triangular pieces extending off the bottom of the quilt. These were originally going to be inserted somehow into the binding and have beads and other dangly things on them. There were also going to be lots more dangly things interspersed in the body of the quilt at irregular intervals. There were going to be beads, ribbons, buttons—just think of all the cool embellishing I could do!

I wish I had a picture of what this might have ended up looking like—frenetic, unfocused, with no place for the eye to rest. Fortunately, my editorial-self stepped in and whispered in my ear, "Less is more." All of those fancy embellishment ideas were discarded in favor of simple lines of colored plastic beads. Why? Just because we CAN do something (and boy, does this apply to more than quilting) doesn't mean we have to. Sometimes, simple is best. The trick to designing a pleasing quilt, even a show-worthy quilt, is knowing how much to include and how much to leave out.

Every facet of a quilt deserves the opportunity to shine. There needs to be a good reason to add more to what is already there. Does the intricate quilting enhance the basic quilt design or does it distract? Does the embellishment serve to highlight certain features or confuse the eye? These are all critical questions to ask oneself as part of the design process.

If I had included all the "extras" that I had envisioned, would the contrasting quilting have really stood out? I don't think so. Would the balance between the rainbow geese and black background have been as stark? Probably not. I will eventually get around to designing a riotous quilt with lots of stuff and bling in it. Each element of that quilt, though, will be included for a reason and make sense in the overall design. Until then, I'll stick with "less is more" and let all the elements speak for themselves.

SOARING TO NEW HEIGHTS
53" x 54"

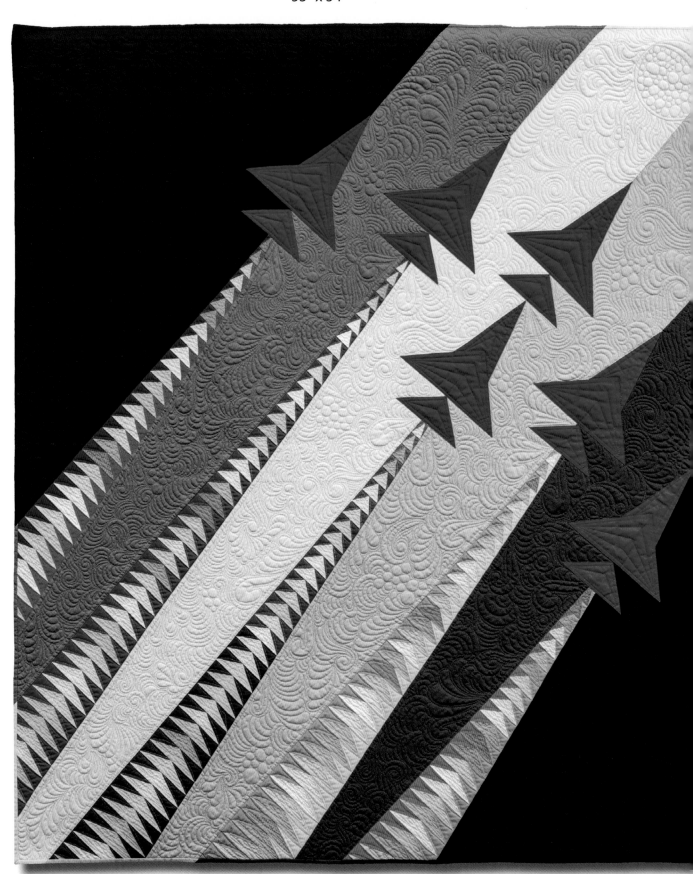

Third Place
COLLEEN ESKRIDGE
Boone, North Carolina
&
JUDY STOKES
Columbus, Mississippi

Colleen

Photo by Bob Eskridge

Judy

Photo by Amy J. Graber

Meet Colleen

I grew up in Sharon, Pennsylvania, the eldest of 15 children. My mother sewed Halloween costumes, but had little time for any other sewing. However, I learned to sew on an old Singer® 99 and made several simple items of clothing on an old Singer treadle machine my dad rescued from the garbage.

My first glimpse of quilting was an exhibit of antique quilts at the Smithsonian Institution and I decided to try this quilting thing. I bought a quilt magazine, cut paper templates, and made a quilt for my little girl out of various colored ginghams. I tied it with yarn. It was very poorly made, but I was proud and she loved it.

Life got in the way, with children, activities, and working. I had lots of starts, plenty of PHDs (Projects Half-Done), but few finishes. In 1994, we moved to Pampa, Texas, where I joined my first quilt guild with a talented group of ladies who kindly shared their knowledge with me. We were down to one child at home and I finally had more time to quilt. More starts and about 70 finishes, mostly baby quilts for all those nieces and nephews. We still had only one quilt in our house made by me though.

In 2004, my husband got an opportunity to work in South Africa for four years and I joined my second quilt guild in Queenstown, South Africa. I decided I would use South African fabrics only, no matter what they were made of, and finally made some quilts for me. The geometric patterns of their fabrics were inspiring to me and I made about 20 quilts while we were there. I even kept a few.

Piecing is fine but I have always been much more interested in the quilting process, whether hand quilting, as in the first 70 baby quilts I made, or machine quilting as I do now. When it came time for us to return to the states, I convinced my husband that if he was going to complete his PhD in public administration, I could get a longarm machine.

Once I had my hand-guided longarm machine, I was completely hooked. We moved to Starkville, Mississippi, and in 2009, I began quilting for myself and for the girls in the local quilt guilds. These women were amazing and pieced very diverse quilts and generously permitted me to quilt their treasures as I saw fit. As I gained confidence, I tried new things I saw on the internet and at quilt shows, which in Mississippi were abundant. My daughter-in-law, Jen Eskridge, a modern quilter, pattern designer, and author, let me do samples and quilts for several of her books. She also introduced me to the modern, graffiti style of quilting.

Quilting the designs into the quilt is my passion. I can do so much more on my machine than I ever could by hand. I love to use lots of fillers on traditional quilts, or cover modern quilts with feathers and swirls. I personally love feathers on my quilts, but enjoy mixing it up to keep it all interesting. I practice new things and ideas on baby quilts and now there are loads of grand-nieces and -nephews to quilt for.

About five years ago I decided to make each of my siblings a bed quilt, I only have two to go. I enjoy making quilts for our eight grandchildren and a few special friends.

About four years ago we moved to Boone, North Carolina, for my husband's job. My guild here does charity quilts and I try to quilt on something several days a week. The majority of my time is spent quilting for my family, friends, and me! You can never have too many quilts and it is therapy for me. I can clear my mind, turn up the radio or CD, and I am transported to another place. In a perfect world I will sew up all

the fabric I have into quilts and get them all quilted in this lifetime! Thankfully, all of my very large family like quilts. Besides siblings, there are about 56 cousins waiting for their quilts. Sew many quilts, sew little time!

I look forward to what can be accomplished this coming year.

Meet Judy

I don't remember a time when I wasn't interested in some type of needlework. Counted cross-stitch was my favorite. Quilting was something I wanted to do . . . one day. When a beginner quilt class was advertised at a local fabric store, I decided to sign up. That way, when I was ready to quilt, I would already know how. That first class was the beginning of my quilt journey. Everything else faded into the background.

I am a scrap quilter who loves traditional quilting. I'm not afraid to learn and try new ideas, but I'm most at home cutting itty-bitty pieces and sewing them back together. I really enjoy participating in mysteries and challenges. I always have several projects going at once. I try to sew, cut out, or fondle fabric every day. It's my relaxation.

I have made quilts for my children and my 21 grandchildren. I want to make more!! I love making the everyday, ordinary quilts, but I always have a vision to make the next show quilt. Whether it wins a ribbon or not, I enjoy the process and the thrill of seeing "my baby" hanging in a show.

I enjoy taking classes. No matter how experienced a quilter becomes, she will always learn something from every class. I also enjoy sharing what I've learned. I've taught several beginner classes. Getting another person as interested in quilting as I am is a true reward.

Inspiration and Design—Colleen

I had never collaborated on a quilt before. But quite truthfully, as I am a poor piecer, it was the only way I would ever have a quilt hanging in Paducah. Judy and I were both members of several quilt guilds when I lived in Mississippi. We live about nine hours from each other now and several states apart, so the back and forth took place mostly in emails, phone calls, and text messages.

Never having taken a quilting class and not using any drawing programs, I am a doodle quilt designer. I draw my ideas, then redraw, sometimes on a white board, sometimes on paper. I sent sketch texts to Judy. Once we had the title, Soaring to New Heights, I began to doodle air current ideas and what I thought wind turbulence might look like on a quilt. I purchased fabrics to test thread colors on to see how they would play with each other. My practice piece for thread colors went on the machine, and I began to doodle with thread. I sent Judy several pictures of the practice piece and asked her what she thought.

After thread choices were made, the design became more alive to me. More sketches, some of which were over the top and far above my expertise to execute, just couldn't be done on the quilt. I lowered my expectations and showed Judy the direction I was heading. With her blessing the quilt was loaded. I have never been so nervous, afraid I would make too many mistakes and ruin Judy's beautiful quilt. The quilt had all that wonderful negative space to fill, but I needed to be careful that the quilting wouldn't overpower her design, which was where choice of thread color helped—texture without too much distraction.

One of the challenges to doing the quilting is that it has to come after the piecing. I hoped that my designs would enhance and lift it, but not totally take over. As I quilted each section, I sent photos for Judy to follow the process and critique. Thankfully, we were both on the same page. When I delivered it to her I was over the moon, though any quilter is probably never totally satisfied with everything. I wished I had changed that or added that. But at some point it has to come off the machine and make way for another quilt. I think I'd like to do this again as it stretched me quite a bit, which can never be a bad thing.

Inspiration and Design—Judy

I originally planned to use curved Flying Geese in my design, and I do plan to make future "geese" quilts trying other designs and layouts. However, a friend

suggested I look at military air show photos, which inspired me to go with the airplane theme. My biggest challenge was choosing fabrics and colors and then actually drawing the Flying Geese patterns.

I asked Colleen if she would consider collaborating with me in making a quilt to enter into the contest. I love to piece quilts but am not very accomplished at quilting. She, on the other hand, says she's just an average piecer but she has the gift to make a quilt come alive with her awesome quilting. Together we make a great team.

I had selected a batik fabric that was originally intended to be the background of the quilt. I made a small practice piece for another challenge to audition the fabrics I had chosen for the NQOF quilt. I soon realized that the batik would not have showcased Colleen's quilting at all! I was so happy I had decided to practice first!

Technique—Judy

I attended a lecture on curved Flying Geese by Sue Rasmussen in 2015. She showed us how she drafts her own paper-piecing patterns to make her geese. Sue had made a small kit for us with the basic items needed and I was hooked! I don't know if I do everything the way she showed us, but she planted the seed and I've let it grow.

I made a sketch of how I wanted the quilt to look.

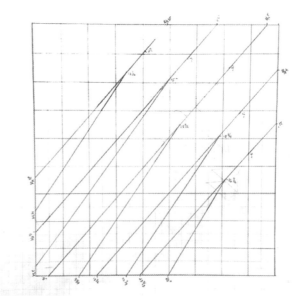

The large pattern base was made from freezer paper taped together to make the size I was going for. To transfer the design, I calculated what percent larger the finished size was from the sketch. I multiplied each measurement on the outside edge of the sketch by this percent and marked the corresponding place on the edge of the large pattern. Then, with a long ruler, I connected the dots. I drew the lines on each of the smoke trails.

I used some pattern tissue I had from my pre-quilting days and traced the design. Using a centering ruler, I marked where the point of each goose would be. Then I drew the geese.

I numbered the pattern pieces and labeled them Fabric Side and Stitching Side so I wouldn't get them accidently reversed. I rolled the pattern up to make it easier to maneuver. I selected the fabrics and precut the pieces, stacking them in the order to be sewn.

I used Ombré by Vanessa Christenson of V and Co. for Moda® fabrics in several colors for the geese. I used mainly Kona® solids for the background of the geese as well as the black and gray background of the quilt. I angled the geese within each strip so when they were added to the background piece there would be straight seams to sew the sections together.

I used HeatnBond® adhesive on the planes and raw-edge appliqué. I also pieced the binding to continue the lines of the quilt. This is the third quilt on which I've used the pieced-binding technique.

I DON'T KNOW IF I'M COMING OR GOING 50½" x 51"

Fourth Place
LESLIE JOHNSON
Arvada, Colorado

Meet Leslie

Photo by Jamey Rabold

My mother always talked about her love of quilts. As a working mother with four children, she didn't get much time to quilt, but she put the "quilting bug" in my head. As a "flower child" of the sixties, I learned some basic sewing, weaving, and crafts.

I decided to make a crazy quilt in about 1970, before quilting had really caught on again. I had no idea what was really involved and no one really taught me, but I made a bunch of squares with a flannel backing, a fluffy batt, and hand stitched crazy quilt designs from fabric scraps on top, sewn together with corduroy sashing and borders, of all things! It was a project that took me many years to complete. When it was finished, we used it until parts were worn to shreds. I discovered I loved quilting!

I started my next quilt about ten years after I started that first one. It was a scrap quilt and this time I learned from books and other quilters. I love that there are so many opportunities for creativity, so many different methods, and so many different ways to use the finished products. I am continuing to learn with every quilt I make. It's a challenge and a pleasure every time.

I recently retired, but my husband was a children's pastor and I had many related responsibilities. I was a teacher at Christian schools for 20 years, then a children's librarian for 15 years. It was difficult to find time to quilt because I was also a mother of three wonderful girls and now a grandmother of four, but I would work on one project at a time, learning more along the way. As I learned, I also had opportunities to join quilt groups, teach basic quilting, and make quilts using a variety of techniques. It was the best way to relax and be productive at the same time.

My mother didn't get a chance to quilt until later in her life, but we all have some of her work in our homes. Her love of quilting sparked an interest in all four of her daughters that continues to this day. My mother, sisters, and I met at AQS QuiltWeek® – Paducah almost every year from 1991 to 2004. After that, the trip got to be too difficult for our mom, but we four sisters continue to meet every year.

We started choosing a project each year and it regularly challenged us to try something new. We have had wonderful times together, working on our projects, laughing, exploring, and catching up on what was happening with our families and in our lives. Since we now live in four different states, it is a pleasant reunion and we will continue to get together, quilt, learn, and stretch our skills and creativity.

Inspiration and Design

I decided to enter the New Quilts from an Old Favorite contest because I loved the idea of working with the Flying Geese pattern. Two of my sisters and I decided to each make a quilt to enter, which made it a lot of fun. When I set to work, I thought I'd look online for quilts that used the pattern, but then I had a flash of inspiration! It just came to mind. I grabbed a piece of paper and started drawing. Within an hour, I had a rough sketch of the quilt that I eventually entered.

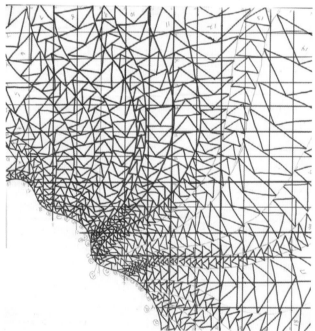

I liked the idea of all different sizes and colors of geese flying out and away from an irregularly shaped corner of the quilt. The movement of the geese would be enhanced by curvature of what I thought of as ribbons. Then I realized there needed to be more geese coming back in, but I wanted them to recede into the background. I decided to make them close to the color of the background fabric. I envisioned a black background to make the colors of the outgoing geese pop. The tone-on-tone geese would add depth to the background.

I started taking fabrics from my stash to see what would work. I had covered my design board with a large piece of dark blue paisley fabric so I could "play" with the colors. I cut triangles and placed them on the design board.

I realized that getting the colors of the geese right would be harder than I thought. I arranged my fabrics according to the color wheel, but had trouble fitting in all the colors until I realized that I wasn't thinking about all the aspects of color (hue, tint, shade, tone, saturation, intensity, and grayscale). I studied these elements of color and put the fabrics on trays so I could work with them in smaller batches. This was the hardest part of designing this quilt.

I put triangles up on the design board (moved into my living room!) and kept my trays handy so I could trade out the ones that didn't seem to work. This continued for weeks. I would go to the trays or to the fabric store to see if I could find the missing piece to complete a ribbon, then go shopping again a week later if I couldn't find what I wanted. I looked at the ribbons on the board in different lights and from different distances until I had them as complete as I thought I could get them.

I kept watching for the perfect fabric for the inbound geese, but couldn't find exactly what I wanted in a black or gray.

Along the way I sent pictures to my sisters, who gave me suggestions. The most important suggestion I received was to use the blue paisley instead of a black fabric for the background. The very interesting, but subtle, design gave more interest and depth to the background. I found a blue fabric for the geese—close to the background fabric but still enough different so the geese would show up. I loved how the colors and the pattern interacted and created the movement of the geese that I was aiming for.

Technique

When I had the plan and the fabrics chosen, I made an actual size pattern on freezer-paper pieces taped together. I used a grid pattern to enlarge my original sketch, making changes as necessary. I copied each ribbon and all the geese on additional freezer-paper strips and used the foundation paper-piecing method to make each ribbon. Visiting my sister while in Paducah for the show, I came across a great blue batik in her stash. I used it for an occasional background goose, just for fun and as a little surprise.

I took the fabric pieces off the design board one ribbon at a time, keeping the triangles in order. I inadvertently reversed the direction of one of the blue geese ribbons. I said out loud that I didn't know if I was coming or going and it became the name of the quilt!

I stabilized each ribbon by basting it on Pellon® 910 interfacing and stitched each ribbon with lines equidistant from each other with rayon thread. I had intended to stitch the same number of lines on each ribbon, but discovered that it was impossible to keep them evenly spaced at the narrow end as well as at the wider end. This photo shows the difficulty with this plan.

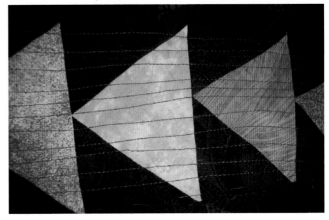

Before

Rather than make the ribbon again, I ripped out all the lines of stitching (Oh, how I hate ripping!), but it was worth the effort.

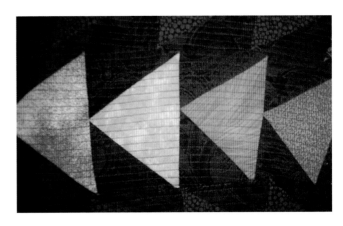

After

This was a difficult part of the project because my threadwork had to go off the edges of each ribbon at irregular intervals. I didn't know how it would look on the finished quilt after I sewed the ribbons together. Each step was an experiment because I had never done anything like this before, nor had I ever seen it done.

Sewing the ribbons together was challenging because of the curved edges. I made registration marks on each edge of each ribbon so I knew how to join them. The biggest challenge came when it was time to add the backing, quilting, and binding. I used Quilters Dream Cotton Request batting because it is thin and lies nice and flat. Because of the curved corner I decided to use the facing method to bind the quilt, and I basted the batting to the quilt top and then stitched the backing on the curved corner first.

After it was turned and pressed, I basted the backing to the batting and top and quilted the layers together, starting at the curved edge and moving out to the four straight outer edges. I was nervous that this would stretch the ribbons, in spite of the stabilizer. I was very careful and used a walking foot and a quilt suspension system so that the weight of the quilt wouldn't pull the ribbons out of shape.

After I finished quilting, I faced the four straight edges. This was an irregular method, but I wasn't sure how to get that curved corner to turn out smoothly. I didn't want a binding because I wanted the geese to appear to fly off the edge of the quilt, so a facing seemed like the only method to make that happen. I did have some small irregularities, but I was able to smooth the quilt and even out the edges without losing the integrity of the design. Success!

JACOB'S PLUMAGE 60" x 68"

Fifth Place
PATRICIA A. HOBBS
Macomb, Illinois

Meet Pat

Photo by John K. Hobbs

I felt honored and thrilled to receive the email stating, "Congratulations, your quilt JACOB'S PLUMAGE has been selected as a finalist in the National Museum's New Quilts from Old Favorites: Flying Geese 2016." A quilter is aware of the time it took to make the quilt and all of the ups and downs along that production journey. Uncertain factors that are a plague to a quilter's thought process come to mind, such as: Is the color scheme right? Is the interpretation of the theme interesting and not too far astray? Maybe the largest doubt of all is: Are my quilting skills good enough for my quilt to be shown for two years out in the quilt world? The acceptance of a quilt into this contest is really a validation of all of the above.

I do love challenges and, after teaching and practicing visual art professionally for over 34 years, I know the design principles and the elements of art. Therefore, I love the process of designing a quilt. Actually making it is the hard part that requires self-discipline.

My relatives, both in Sweden and in the United States, have successfully pursued their professional careers in art, architecture, or engineering. My family's endeavors have greatly influenced my professional artistic development. After retiring from teaching, while simultaneously producing professional watercolors, I was attracted to the fiber arts.

If you look back into my childhood, I was designing by the age of nine. My cousin and I used newspapers to make some lovely Hawaiian outfits to be worn around her farmhouse. Growing up, I considered being a cowgirl, fashion designer, ballerina, book illustrator, dollmaker, artist, and teacher. In reality, I have done most of these.

Pat (left) with her cousin, Judy Hull. Photo by her aunt, Forna Flager.

I still paint and show watercolors and enjoy painting with my *Plein Air* group. We go out into nature and paint the scenery. Just when I think I am finished repairing and dressing antique dolls, someone will ask me to fix and dress their doll. The last doll restoration began with only a dilapidated head. The rest of the time in the last two years I have spent making installations for the local art center windows, painting murals, and doing freelance work.

My husband has said that my motto should be, "I quilt; therefore, I am." I quilt and sew in a very small room, usually from 10:30 p.m. to 12:30 a.m. That still gives me time to do all of my housekeeping and have a life. I started sewing at age 10 and have worn out two sewing machines in my lifetime. Last year I won a sewing machine in the 30th Anniversary of Dogwoods contest in Paducah, Kentucky.

Another quilt challenge that I participated in this year was Fly Me to the Moon in honor of the upcoming anniversary of the lunar landing and man's first walk on the moon. This was sponsored and directed by Susanne Jones. After she posted her idea, there were artists from eight countries registered to make 179 quilts. Selected quilts may be seen at www.flymetothemoon.gallery. My entry was THE MOON IN THE CLASSROOM.

Most of all, I enjoy the process of creativity. It's what keeps my mind active and is a way of life for me.

Inspiration and Design

My inspiration came from the challenge of the contest itself. I love challenges. The theme of Flying Geese brought many visions to mind. My high school art teacher suggested that one should begin a project by listing ideas associated with the theme, trying to think outside of the box.

I don't do a great quantity of traditional machine piecing. Instead I prefer appliqué by hand for quilt construction. I imagined the triangle pieces represent the triangle flight pattern of geese during migration. This piecing had to be included on the quilt somewhere, somehow.

None of my ideas seemed too difficult to make, but I tried to be realistic about the time needed to execute my different design ideas.

Idea number one included the highway leading into Paducah using perspective. I really wanted to use the image of the bridge located outside of Paducah as

its girders are in a Flying Geese format. It would have been enjoyable to make, as I like pictorial and realistic designs. My idea was to make a transition from the geometric bridge girders into realistic flying geese.

Idea number two was a large circle of pieced triangular Flying Geese moving from large to a smaller size. Simultaneously the triangles of the bridge would turn into realistic geese flying off from the circle. As in the first design idea, there was no smooth transition from the bridge to the geese. On this idea sketch there was a goose showing pieced wings with triangles. That was the first glimpse of the goose used in the final design.

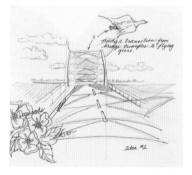 

Idea number three was a close-up of the bridge and geese in a formation that almost looked like an M.C. Escher tessellation. The design just didn't make any sense. None of the designs that included the image of the bridge worked as interesting compositions. Collaging bits and pieces of a composition is like putting a puzzle together. When finished, the picture plane needs to look cohesive, with all of the parts belonging to the whole design and composition. I believe that traditional geometric quilt patterns need to be included in a quilt design as they add texture, life, and interest to a realistic scene. They are easily recognizable and become a visual comfort zone.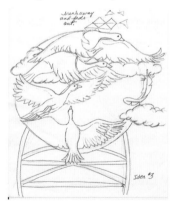

When the final design idea was being drafted, I researched geese photos. I have childhood memories of being chased by the meanest of geese in my uncle's barnyard, but there needed to be more acuteness when drawing the geese images. I also looked at photos of feathers and goose down. I thought I could easily draw a feather, but it never hurts to see a real feather floating down on air currents.

I wanted to appliqué a couple of feathers onto the quilt and quilt some in the outer border. To balance the composition, I put a large goose egg in one corner and joked to a friend that I hoped the quilt wouldn't lay an egg.

Construction Techniques

The idea for my design included a couple of images that appeared in some of my earlier drawn designs. The large goose image was okay the first way I had drawn it except for the head. A goose's head seems small in proportion to its body. I scanned my drawing and used the grid in Adobe® software to divide the design into 30 equal rectangles. As I printed each rectangle, I enlarged it to 8" x 10". This method controlled the proportions so that each rectangle fit together smoothly after printing and left enough border to overlap the pieces. I worked in rows, left to right. If I didn't tape them together immediately, I numbered the rectangles (row 1a; row 1b; etc.) making sure the orientation was correct. Then I redrew the head and glued it into place.

I had already picked out the background fabric, Caryl Bryer Fallert-Gentry's fabric by Moda that mimics her hand-dyed ombré fabric. There was just one problem. I had purchased only one yard of it. To extend this fabric to be large enough to meet the 50" wide requirement, strips in varying widths of a coordinating striped fabric were set into the background

A large white appliquéd domestic goose would be the main image. This goose was broken down into its component parts. The outstretched wing was made first by using tracing paper to copy the original drawing. Each large wing feather was cut apart from the tracing paper. I drew the traditional Flying Geese triangles onto the tracing paper to be used to machine paper piece. It was necessary to do each wing feather separately as the triangles were different sizes. The head and feet were made next, and then the body.

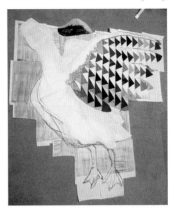

There is a small amount of DecoArt® SoSoft® fabric paint used to put shading on the goose. The parts of the goose were laid out on the original pattern to check their sizes. The goose was sewn onto the background using a combination of needle-turn hand appliqué and machine raw-edge appliqué. Extra fabric was trimmed out from under the appliqué.

Another gray partial goose, an egg, and three feathers were appliquéd on or near the large blue-green border. Later I thought that I should have added a line of rainbow-colored goslings somewhere on the quilt.

This is a good reason why artists do series of a work or piece making subtle changes on each ensuing piece. Instead, I painted a stripe of traditional Flying Geese down one side. I didn't like the way the large wings looked, so I hand sewed an ⅛" wide binding down the centers of the triangles and added beading.

The large blue-green border was machine quilted with realistic feathers using the downy parts to continue moving from one feather to the next. The label on the back is in the shape of a goose footprint and holds the quilt's pertinent information.

ON THE WINGS OF ETERNITY
51" x 65½"

Finalist
JEAN BRUEGGENJOHANN
Columbia, Missouri

Meet Jean

Photo by James W. Reese

My grandmother, a needleworker extraordinaire, taught me to embroider when I was five or six years old. I did not like it much, and I vowed to never waste my time doing it again. My mother was an excellent self-taught seamstress who made beautiful clothes, especially very fancy mini-skirted dresses that she wore to dances in the 1960s. These were very special, with velvet, satin, and other luxurious fabrics that she highly embellished with rhinestones and other opulent trims. She taught me to sew on a portable Singer® sewing machine when I was nine or 10. Once I learned to sew, I made a lot of my own clothes. I think my mother's beautiful dresses are why I have a great love and affinity for glitzy, sparkly embellishments of all kinds.

I took a hiatus from sewing for over a decade in the late 1970s and early 1980s. I moved multiple times, changed jobs, and had two children. After moving to a new neighborhood, I took a quilting class nearby just for fun. I did not know anything about quilting, but it immediately became a passion. I am a professional graphic designer and professor of art and everything about quilting spoke to me about the designs that I had been creating for decades. I continued to take classes then, and I still take classes when I can find the time.

ON THE WINGS OF ETERNITY is the fifth quilt I have made using similar fabrics, design elements, flowers, or landscapes, and are all heavily embellished This particular body of work has been very exciting for me to make. I am a learner and very happy when there is a problem to solve, and my most recent quilts have provided me with plenty of problems. One problem was that one quilt required embroidery and I needed to learn how to embroider! My six-year-old self had pledged never to do it again, but here I was signing up for an embroidery class! I found that I really liked it! It was another problem solved and a new skill learned.

Every time I make a quilt I learn more about color, contrast, and design using fabric, and also technical skills such as different ways to bond and adhere fabric and raw-edge appliqué. My beading skills have improved from working on these embellished quilts.

All the work that I design and produce is original. I belong to a quilt guild and several mini groups and I find that I pick up ideas, inspiration, and techniques at almost every meeting. All of my work is done in my studio, and I like to spend time there thinking, listening to music, reading, and sewing. I keep track of what I want to work on in a sketchbook, and it is filled with past and future projects. I finally started keeping organized boxes with all my patterns and large full-size sketches so I can go back and review techniques and designs.

My plan for the future is to try to create some "modern" quilts. As I think about how to approach this new type of quilt, the most important thing I have to consider is how to introduce the glitz and high embellishment that will have to be part of these quilts.

Inspiration and Design

This quilt has to do with resurrection, love, joy, beauty, eternity, continuity, serendipity, fearlessness, and the lightness of being. The hummingbird symbolizes all these things. It is about living in the moment; it is captivating and beguiling, believing anything is possible. The jungle is an entity unto itself— a living character or being similar to the hummingbird and fish—and the shafts of light that illuminate the center are hope—an implacable force. I wanted the quilt to have mists and swirling wisps (vapors) and enchanted creatures coming together to celebrate the hummingbird. As I worked on this quilt I always thought of it as the "dark and scary quilt with the hopeful beams of light."

I have made many quilts and the longer I make them, the more I want them to be conceptually strong. I want the form and images to be driven by the idea, so I spent a lot of time thinking about this quilt. It is probably the last in this particular series, and I wanted it to be different and the most elaborate. I wanted all of its parts to be as dimensional as possible. I have stuffed and beaded insects, layers that are transparent, fancy bedazzled fabric, embroidery, bronze wire, beads, and stones. I wanted to push the materials and what I did with them as far as I could. These different materials led to a lot of problems and problem solving, something I really enjoy.

The last design consideration for this quilt was how to infuse it with Flying Geese, one of my favorite patterns. The thing that I like most about this contest is that I get to couple a traditional quilt pattern with anything else I want to do. I love traditional quiltmaking, and I almost always include some nod to the traditions that have come before in my quilts.

Here I used a one-patch color wash in the background with horizontal and vertical lines of Flying Geese embedded throughout my color wash of squares.

I used Flying Geese in my machine appliquéd round flowers and in my swirling wisps (vapors).

Once I had the idea and a direction in terms of materials, I started to make pencil sketches. I drew plants that I knew: palm trees, bird of paradise, and other tropicals. I knew I wanted to have a water feature so I could have a leaping fish and dragonflies. The concept and design came fairly easily for this quilt. The making of it did not. Many times I thought something would work, a design or color, and it would not; so it seemed like everything was a real struggle. However, overcoming each struggle made this quilt more important to me because I could see each problem solved.

I would say that I am very happy with this quilt. It came out very much like I thought in my original thinking of the concept.

TECHNIQUE

I design all my work as small pencil sketches about 4" x 6" and blow them up on a large printer to full size. On this quilt, I used a true size print to make all of my patterns with tracing paper and newsprint. I designed the color-wash background single block by single block to get the colors and values right, then started on the plants, trees, and animal life. That was the easy part. The hard part on this quilt was figuring out the color, value, and fabric.

I can't even begin to count the number of fabrics used in this quilt! I spent time thinking about and planning how I wanted the contrast to work. This was difficult because I had multiple layers on the foreground and more on the background that changed from light to dark. I also had an abstracted lower (ground level) part of the quilt, then deep jungle, lighter for the shaft of light, and finally darker where the abstract canopy of the jungle came together at the top. All of this shifting background made it very difficult to visualize. I tried sketching it, but quickly gave up because it was so complex.

I finally decided to just start and go with the best decision I could make at the time. My philosophy was to go with the highest contrast possible. I figured even if the color was crazy, such as my red bird of paradise plant, at least it would stand out from the background if the contrast was great enough. It worked.

Then I only had to worry about the scale of the patterns in the fabric that I put next to each other. I have been working with color all my life as a graphic designer, but working with fabric has exponentially increased my color expertise.

Once I finished piecing and sewing the quilt top, the quilting became a challenge. I really wanted the quilting to make its presence known. I used leaf and plant patterns and other organic shapes to add to the overall design and create an extra layer of complexity to the jungle. I took more chances using contrasting colors in the quilting so it showed up more. This also was successful and it gave me confidence to do more and push the colors more.

When I go to the fabric store, I often go with no idea what I will buy. I rarely can visualize what I need, but I can often identify what I need when I see it. One day I came home with some variegated yellow/green fabric that was loosely woven, so you could see through it and it sparkled. I wasn't exactly sure what I would do with it, but I thought, "Why not get a bit of it?" It became my palm tree fronds. I went through numerous designs and different fabric and nothing worked until I tried the variegated sparkly fabric and it was perfect. This is how a lot of my work gets done.

In general, when I make a quilt, I always have a plan, a sketch, color and embellishment ideas, my technical skills, and my love of working. I think my success comes from being flexible and open to new skills and decision-making. I am sure I will make quilts all my life.

WELKOM NEDERLAND 58½" x 56½"

Finalist
TERE D'AMATO
Mashpee, Massachusetts

Meet Tere

Photo by Lori Whalen

Twenty years ago, I made my first quilt and my creative life has been expanding ever since. I remember attending my first quilting conference; like a puppy, my nose explored every corner of the venue. I took eleven classes over four days and skipped lunch to explore the vendor booths. Eager to learn every aspect of quilting, I tried hand quilting, fabric dyeing, beadwork, appliqué, foundation piecing, and embroidery. Soon I needed bookshelves and storage units to hold my new treasures. And the fabric stash I accumulated, oh my!

When it came time to retire, there was no doubt how I would spend my days. But first we had to find a new home with space for my quilting and my husband's photography pursuits. We found just the right home on Cape Cod.

There is no place I would rather be than in my quilting studio. It is a place to gather friends to share our latest quilting projects. The studio invariably attracts the grandchildren, so I always have a kid-friendly sewing machine, scraps, and art supplies at hand. It is also a quiet retreat where I spend hours quilting, accompanied by my soft-coated wheaten terrier, Hermione.

2016 brought an exciting new venture into my quilting life, thanks to my friend Carol Duffy. Let me tell you about her.

I met Carol several years ago in a class sponsored by our local guild. Our class project was the intricate foundation pieced Bali Wedding Ring bed runner designed by Judy Niemeyer. We spent two days preparing the components and only managed to sew one ring. Thinking this could be just another UFO, I asked my tablemates to come to my studio the following week. Over the next couple of months, the presence of my new friends provided me the incentive to finish my bed runner.

It was lovely to look at but all I could think was, "Why, oh why, didn't I take risks like Carol?" Her color choices were dramatic, the quilting designs intricate, and the piped binding on the scalloped border expertly executed. Carol's Wedding Ring quilt went on to win ribbons and recognition around the country. I knew I had to "up my game" to catch up to my new friend.

Over the years we have served as each other's muse, and we both have grown exponentially in our skills and creativity. So, when Carol threw out the suggestion that we collaborate on our own line of patterns, I agreed. I was already knee-deep working on WELKOM NEDERLAND but if you love quilting, you've got to love even more quilting. After nine months of designing and testing, we rolled out our Summerhouse Block of the Month to enthusiastic response. We are already planning our next series. Quilting has never been so much fun.

Inspiration

The borders of WELKOM NEDERLAND tell the story of my family trip to Holland in 2015. Landing in Amsterdam, I at once felt at home. The city is immensely walkable yet has more bicycles than residents. I soon learned I was more likely to be wiped out by a cyclist than by a car when crossing a street. You must take a glass-topped boat tour along the interlocking canals to really appreciate the city's unique architecture and charm. The countryside outside Amsterdam is pancake-flat, making it easy to explore by rented bicycle, headwinds and other challenges notwithstanding.

Our rented apartment was in the southern canal district close to the museums, zoos, and parks. The museum district is where I saw the Delftware *tulipieres*, large vases with "spouts" to hold tulip bulbs. In the 1600s, tulips, hyacinths, and crocuses were considered luxury items and tulipieres were designed to show off your wealth and status as evidenced by the flowers you could display.

I was on the lookout for Flying Geese designs during our travels. The triangle quilt block showed up everywhere—on the house shutters, windmill blades, even as boat sails. I had plenty of ideas for starting my quilt. But first I wanted to find a much-loved book from my childhood called *Tales Told in Holland,* published in 1926, edited by Olive Beaupre Miller and illustrated by Maud and Miska Petersham. As a child, I would trace and color the illustrations long before I could read its words. Returning home, I found it

archived on the Internet. You can see my inspiration for WELKOM NEDERLAND on the book's endpapers.

I hid twenty-one Flying Geese blocks in the border of my quilt. Can you find them?

Technique

I start my design process by roughly sketching ideas on graph paper. Initially, I envisioned a center panel featuring a boy flying a kite, but no matter how I scaled the design, the kite did not give me a dominant visual anchor to offset all that was going on in the borders. Instead, I created an updated version of a tulipiere and filled it with rich red tulips. A circle of Flying Geese was stitched in heavy red thread behind the vase during the quilting stage.

Once satisfied with the composition, it was time to create a full-size drawing. The Internet was my resource for Dutch architecture, and windmill and animal images. When I found a shape that appealed to me, I traced its outline from the screen of my iPad. There is no need for detail as this can be added through the choice of fabric. Next I drew my city and village buildings on graph paper and copied them several times along my borders. Once the master was done, I copied the pattern one more time onto Golden Threads Quilting Paper. This gave me an overlay for positioning appliqué units.

Because the dimensions of the center and borders depended on the size of my inner Flying Geese border, I attacked this element first. A Bloc Loc® Flying Geese ruler made this step easy. It is so accurate and easy.

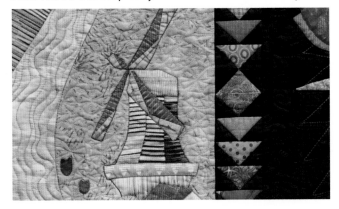

I pieced the background fabric for the borders using a technique I learned from Ricky Tims. Trace your border's background onto freezer-paper. For instance, the background of my right border consists of a grassy field, a curved bicycle path, a dike, and a body of water.

Before cutting the pattern apart, make tick marks across the piecing lines; number or label the pieces on both the master pattern and the freezer-paper templates. It also helps to mark grainlines. Cut apart the freezer-paper pattern and iron a section to the fabric, right-side up. Roughly cut the fabric approximately ¼" larger than the freezer-paper pattern, then staystitch a few threads width away from the edge of the freezer paper all around. Matching the tick marks, pin adjoining pieces together and sew just within the staystitching. Clip inner curves if necessary and press the seams to one side.

For the appliquéd elements, I used the recently discovered Appliquick® tools, a set of two metal wands, one with a spatula-shaped tip and the other with a fork-shaped tip. In conjunction with a special stabilizer, the tools allow you to easily turn appliqué seam allowances.

After cutting the appliqué shape from the stabilizer, tack it to your fabric and cut out with a $^3/_{16}$" seam allowance. Using the Appliquick fork tip to hold the tiny piece in place, lightly apply glue to the seam allowances. Using the spatula-shaped end, fold the seam allowance over the stabilizer edges. Allow to dry and you are ready to machine appliqué. I used a tiny zigzag with 100-wt. silk or InvisiFil® thread in matching colors.

You don't have to remove the stabilizer as it will soften the first time it is wet. After the quilt was completed, I soaked it to remove the glue and starch. I don't prewash my commercial fabrics as I starch them before cutting and this usually identifies fabric that bleeds. I had very little color migration; but where it happened, dabbing it with a damp Shout® ColorCatcher® sheet lifted the offending dye.

Time for the quilting! I recently purchased a sit-down longarm machine and finally have enough room to use double batting. The layer next to the backing is Quilters Dream Request, a very thin cotton batting. On top is a layer of Quilters Dream wool batting. This combo allowed my appliqué to puff nicely while helping the quilt hang straight.

The last step is one of my favorite parts—sewing on the binding. I recently watched Susan Cleveland on Craftsy apply a piped binding and just had to try it. Based on her directions, it was surprisingly simple and added just the right finishing touch. My friend Carol digitized a tulipiere embroidery design for me, perfect for my one-of-a-kind label.

DESTINATION UNKNOWN 59" x 59"

Finalist
MARY KAY DAVIS
Sunnyvale, California

Meet Mary Kay

Photo by Clayton Davis

Like many of my contemporaries, I began sewing as a child. My mother gave me a needle and thread and I made clothes for my dolls. In junior high, I had to take the obligatory sewing class, but it wasn't until my mother had me take sewing lessons that I began to make my own clothes. My mother was a smart woman; even though she was a wonderful seamstress, I noticed that she asked me to make more and more of her clothes. I think that was her plan all along when she had me take those lessons.

Quilting didn't take part in my life until I was almost forty years old. While my mother sewed clothes, no one in the family had anything to do with quilting. I just happened to walk into my neighborhood quilt shop one day looking for fabric and decided to take a "quilt-as-you-go" class. I took it very literally and thought I had to have the whole quilt finished by the end of four classes. I used templates, hand pieced, hand appliquéd, machine appliquéd, and hand quilted that quilt by the end of the 8-week session. I am surprised I ever quilted again.

From then on, there was no looking back. I made a quilt for my brother's birthday, my mother-in-law's birthday, as wedding gifts, and as baby gifts. The quilt bug had hit me. I joined the local guild and designed their opportunity quilt. I was the featured quilter at their biannual quilt show. I donated quilts to my children's schools. I also began working at the quilt shop where I first took that class—the Granary in Sunnyvale, California. Then I began teaching classes and speaking at other guilds.

I started entering quilt challenges and one of them would change my life. In 2005, I entered the P&B Textiles/Alex Anderson Morning Garden Challenge. This was a national challenge and I ended up winning the Grand Prize with my quilt EXPLOSION OF DELIGHT. Part of the prize was having lunch with Alex Anderson and Irwin Bear (President of P&B Textiles). As a result of that luncheon, I was invited by Alex to contribute my quilt CRÈME BRULEÉ to her next book, *Neutral Essentials*, and then I was asked to do more.

EXPLOSION OF DELIGHT

CRÈME BRULEÉ

In 2007, Alex teamed up with Ricky Tims to create the website www.TheQuiltShow.com. The site has true TV-quality shows where they bring you top quilters from around the world. The site is all about education, and they have classes, newsletters, a daily blog, and more. This is where I come in; I am currently the newsletter creator/editor, blog creator, and part-time photographer for the site—all because I entered Alex's challenge in 2005.

As you can see, I still enjoy entering challenges—mostly because I'd never get anything done if I didn't have a deadline. I also create patterns for Blend Fabrics and Anna Griffin, and on occasion I still work at The Granary. I also have a website, www.ThreadsontheFloor.com.

I lost my wonderful husband in February 2012 and have found that quilting, along with my two delightful sons, keeps me busy and fulfilled.

Inspiration and Design

DESTINATION UNKNOWN is an apt title for this quilt. When I started it, I wasn't really sure what I wanted to do or how the quilt would actually look when it was finished. There were only two things I knew for sure. One, the quilt would contain Flying Geese; and two, I really wanted to use some Jane Sassaman fabric I had been hoarding. It turns out only one of those things actually happened.

I loved the colors and designs in Jane Sassaman's fabric lines Strawberry Serenade and Butterfly Garden. I thought I would pull the colors out and then use the prints from the fabric as either setting squares or borders.

Well, I did pull out the colors, but when I started laying out the quilt, I just couldn't see a way to incorporate the prints. I didn't want to add borders just for the sake of adding borders. Since I was using fabrics that "read as solids," it seemed that the quilt was becoming very graphic, and adding the print seemed to muddle it up. So my lovely fabric has made its way back into my stash for use on another day.

Another design concern was the modification of the Flying Geese block. I knew I wanted to make some variation, but still wanted to make it recognizable as a Flying Geese block. I ended up simplifying a block I had created for a previous quilt, SHIFTING FOCUS. In that original block, there were eight additional black Flying Geese. I removed these to simplify the block. I call it the Decreasing Geese block.

SHIFTING FOCUS

In the Decreasing Geese block, the geese shrink in size and are not contained within the traditional rectangle. They are set into a more trapezoidal shape. These geese all follow the same path. In the second block, the geese are in a more traditional setting. However, in this block, the geese follow their own paths. The final block is a Checkerboard Nine Patch. Not all blocks can fly.

Only these three blocks are used in DESTINATION UNKNOWN.

The challenge with all the blocks was in their size. As each block is 7" finished, some of the pieces were very small. I ended up paper piecing the Decreasing Geese block and used strip piecing where possible in the other two blocks. I also chain pieced as much as I could to keep things in order.

There were a lot of pieces and a lot of points. One thing I learned: Never stop to count the pieces! It can slow you down and make you fear you will never finish.

Because I was not entirely clear about what I was making, I began the quilt using only fabrics that I had in my stash, which presented another challenge. Many of them were out of print, and I ran out of both the black print and the neon green print. I decided to accept these problems as design "opportunities" instead.

For the black, I substituted solid black for the setting triangles and quilted those areas in a similar design to the print. For the neon green print, I found a solid that I felt worked quite well.

I wanted a binding that would add pizzazz without detracting too much from the graphic design. I serendipitously came across a bias-striped fabric with similar colors to my quilt. Sometimes you just have to dig deep into your stash to find what you what.

What I really like about the quilt is that by using only three blocks, a number of secondary patterns are formed. It all depends on where you rest your eye. If you look at the center, you can see a circular shape. If you cast your eye more to the side, you see four other circular shapes. By concentrating on the straight lines, you see squares. This is not a restful quilt; it is full of motion. The use of bright "solids" creates quite a visual impact.

Technique

Here is the paper-piecing pattern for the Decreasing Geese block. When printed, the block should measure 7½" to the outside line. It is a 7" finished block.

There are many ways to paper piece. For the actual sewing, I use the stitch-and-flip method; but when it comes to cutting out the pieces, I'm usually in a hurry and prefer to cut out just squares and rectangles. This way, I'm always sure that enough fabric will cover the area of the block being sewn. There is nothing worse than cutting out a piece of fabric too small and not discovering it until you have already "stitched and flipped." This method allows me to not worry about cutting out odd shapes, only squares and rectangles. It also makes it much easier for me to determine how much fabric I need.

What do I mean by cutting only squares and rectangles? I measure each section of the block and then cut an over-sized square or rectangle to cover the area. For example, for piece A10, I used a clear acrylic ruler to determine that a 1¾" square would work to cover the area. I knew that I needed 36 squares 1¾" for the quilt, so I divided the width of the fabric, in this case 42", by the size of the square, 1¾", so I knew that I could get 24 squares from a 1¾" strip of fabric. I then cut two 1¾" strips by the width of the fabric (WOF) and then subcut them into the 36 squares that I needed.

When placing the ruler on top of the area to be measured, I made sure to include enough fabric for a ¼" seam allowance. I used this method for pieces A10, A7, A4, and A1, using squares or rectangles as necessary (fig, 1, page 51).

For one block you'll need:
A10 = 1¾" square
A7 = 2¼" x 3⅜" rectangle
A4 = 2⅞" x 5⅜" rectangle
A1 = 3⅛" x 7⅞" rectangle

For the side triangles A8, A5, and A2, I measured the pieces at an angle (fig. 2, page 51).
A8/A9 = 2⅝" x 1⅛" rectangle
A5/A6 = 1⅝" x 3⅝" rectangle
A2/A3 = 2⅛" x 5⅛" rectangle

I made an exception when I cut the pieces for A11 and A12. For these I cut 5" x 9" rectangles and then cut them in half diagonally. Some had to be cut left to right and some had to be cut right to left. Two rectangles yielded enough for two blocks.

For the second Flying Geese block, I used the following for each block:

A = 2⅜" squares cut diagonally. Cut 4 squares of each color for a total of 8 half-square triangles per color.
B = 3⅝" x 1¼" rectangles. Cut 4 black.
C = 1¼" square. Cut 1 purple.
D = 2" squares cut diagonally. Cut 8 squares to make 1 block for a total of 16 half-square triangles.

For the Checkerboard Nine Patch, I used the following for each block:

A = 2⅞" squares. Cut 4 from blue.
B = 2⅞" x 1¼" rectangles. Cut 8 from black and 4 from green.
C = 1¼" squares. Cut 4 from pink, 4 from blue, and 1 from green.

The block can be made using the pieces cut individually using these measurements or it can be strip pieced.

Cut two 1¼" wide by WOF black strips.
Cut one 1¼" wide by WOF green strip.
Sew these 3 strips together into a strip-set.
Subcut 4 segments 2⅞" wide for each block.

The same method can be used to create the Checkerboard center.

Cut two 1¼" x WOF blue strips.
Cut three 1¼" x WOF pink strips.
Cut one 1¼" x WOF green strip.
Make 2 blue/pink/blue strip-sets.
Make 1 pink/green/pink strip-set.
Subcut 1¼" segments.
Join these segments to create the center of the block.

Make as many of the blocks as you like, and then have fun laying them out. Rotate the blocks, change the colors, leave out some blocks entirely, or use solid blocks. Just keep playing—your Destination is Unknown!

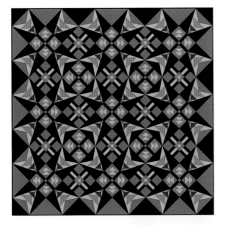

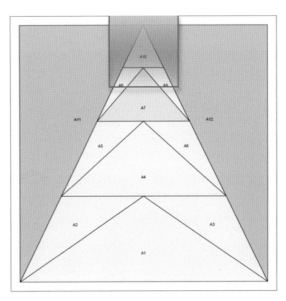

Figure 1

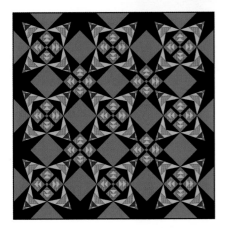

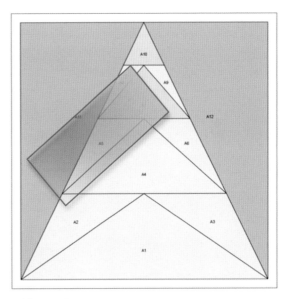

Figure 2

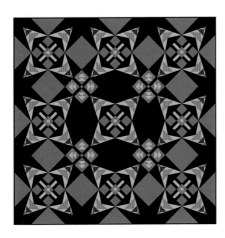

CELEBRATION 65" x 65"

Finalist

GAIL GARBER

Rio Rancho, New Mexico

&

KRIS VIERRA

Lincoln, Nebraska

Gail

Kris

Inspiration

CELEBRATION was born from a drawing that I did many years ago, when I was experimenting with diagonal elements in a medallion-style quilt. That drawing sat there for years before I rediscovered it, although the original was much simpler and smaller than the final rendition. As with many of my quilts, I retreated to my cabin in the Jemez Mountains to begin intensive work on the quilt top. My companions in that adventure were the Hawks Aloft educational Ferruginous Hawk and my two dogs, Gabby and Laney.

Expanding and creating more depth and intricacy in the Flying Geese, arranged in opposing rows, became the greatest stitching challenge in matching all the points.

It's hard to identify my favorite parts of CELEBRATION because I really like the quilt as a whole. It is a happy quilt! Certainly, the "bubbles" add to the design, but I also love the checkerboard in the center of the quilt. I also worked hard to shade the background fabrics from light to dark to create the illusion of light in the center of the quilt.

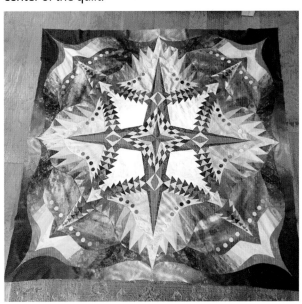

Usually, each of my quilts is quite different from past ones; however, two elements have greatly intrigued me and certainly will show up in future quilts. In fact, the tiny bubbles are used to embellish my newer quilt, SOMETHING FISHY THIS WAY COMES, and I expect circles to be prominently featured in coming years, as will the checkerboard. In general, I have a love of bright colors, hand-dyed gradations, and hand-painted fabrics. They are ageless in that they can't be pin-pointed to any one style or generation of fabric, making it difficult to date a quilt made with them.

Meet Gail

Bold, colorful, and stunning geometric designs with Flying Geese galore—that's how you know you're looking at one of Gail's quilts! Her style has become immediately recognizable because of her talent for combining vivid colors with intricate piecework. Her geometric star quilts and pictorial quilts have won awards at shows throughout the United States and have been featured in publications worldwide. Students love her ability to make these designs achievable, even for novice quilt designers.

Author of three books and more than 100 magazine articles, Gail judges quilt shows, conducts workshops, and lectures throughout the United States and abroad. Her workshops range from novice-level classes that take the mystery out of paper-foundation techniques and curved-seam piecing to intermediate classes focusing on original design.

Her quilting career began innocently enough when her friends talked her into taking a quilting class, thinking that she might enjoy the craft. Little did Gail, or anyone else, suspect that it would become her great passion—one that continues to this day, 37 years later. Quilting also opened many avenues for Gail, some of which could never have been predicted. It was through the design and creation of a raffle quilt for a local birding organization back in the 1980s that led her to also pursue a career in avian conservation and the founding of Hawks Aloft, Inc., in Albuquerque, New Mexico, in 1994.

Today, Gail manages a staff of ten, including biologists, educators, wildlife rehabilitators, and a team of about 70 volunteers, all working together to protect all species of birds and their habitats. One of her very special joys is working with the 25+ permanently injured, non-releasable raptors that form the centerpiece of their extensive, statewide educational outreach program.

AQS QuiltWeek® – Albuquerque 2015 featured the retrospecitve exhibit "From the Land of Enchantment: Thirty Years of Quilts by Gail Garber." Her first effort, AZIMUTH, is a king-size medallion-style quilt that features a Mariner's Compass in the center and variations of the compass throughout the quilt. This award-winning quilt has been displayed at quilt venues throughout the United States and overseas. It is now in the collection of The National Quilt Museum in Paducah, Kentucky, along with another of Gail's signature quilts, COSMIC PARADE, which was featured on the cover of her second book, *Stellar Journeys*.

Meet Kris

Kris has been a quilter/seamstress for more than 20 years and a professional longarm quilter for nine. She teaches throughout the United States and has won numerous national awards for her machine quilting skills. Her most recent work can be seen on the album art for the Australian band the Avalanches' new album "WildFlower." She also runs a full-time longarm quilting business and is designing her own line of longarm rulers and wholecloth quilt stencils.

Techniques

Like nearly all of my recent quilts, all of the pieced sections were stitched using freezer-paper foundation piecing. I love freezer paper because, when pressed, the fabric adheres to the waxy side of the paper, securing all the pieces firmly in place. The only piece of fabric that is loose is the one being attached. All the curved seams were assembled using standard curved-seam piecing techniques.

CELEBRATION features mostly hand-dyed gradations and hand-painted fabrics. Other background fabrics were hand painted by Mickey Lawler, of SkyDyes. I love her fabrics! Some of the background fabrics were hand dyed especially for this quilt. My goal was to have the illusion of light in the center of the quilt, fading to dark on the edges.

Once the pieced portion of the top was complete, it seemed to me to be a little more linear than desired. I hand-appliquéd the gradation bubbles using Karen Kay Buckley's Perfect Circles® templates. It was great fun to add the unexpected element in CELEBRATION.

Kris longarm quilted it in patterns of her own design, working her special magic on the quilt.

Kris has this to say about her artistry: "The quilting was inspired by the design of the quilt. I incorporated curved crosshatching and feathers to accent and highlight the unique piecing and appliqué circles. Gold and blue thread was used to blend with and show off the gradated fabrics."

TWIRLY BIRDS 50" x 50"

Finalist

JULIA GRABER

Brooksville, Mississippi

Meet Julia

Photo by Amy J. Graber

I was born and raised in the beautiful Shenandoah Valley of Virginia along the banks of the North River in Bridgewater. I come from a family of seven sisters and one brother. We spent many happy hours roaming the woods and swimming in the river when our chores were all done. Now that we have all married and have families of our own, we like to get together for a week to ten days for a retreat. We sew, quilt, talk, laugh, relax, and take turns fixing meals. We take our current projects and work on them, learning and gaining inspiration from each other.

I moved to Mississippi to teach school and it was there that I met and married Paul Graber. We have five boys and one girl and now enjoy 12 grandchildren. We live on a farm near Brooksville growing cotton and grains, raising hogs, and are involved in a small trucking company. We are members of Magnolia Mennonite Church and enjoy the fellowship and activities of our local brotherhood as well as mission activities in Romania.

I made a few utility-type quilts soon after

we were married and as the children were growing up. It wasn't until after our youngest went to school that I really delved into making quilts, taking up the challenge of designing my own. In time I have taught quiltmaking classes and fiber art classes in my home and at surrounding guilds. My love for the craft has grown with each quilt.

When the Possum Town Quilters of Columbus, Mississippi, formed a guild in 2004, I joined as a charter member. They have provided me with lots of inspiration, encouragement, and challenges. I'm also a member of AQS and have served as president of Mississippi Quilter's Association, and as a co-rep for Studio Art Quilt Associates of which I am a juried artist member.

I still like the traditional and scrappy large quilts, but recently I have been drawn to making smaller works in fiber, creating art quilts. I love the challenge of taking an image, whether from a photograph, nature, or my mind, and creating it with fabric and thread. My fiber art work is representational and often with minimum detail. It brings me joy when viewers of my work are drawn in for a closer look. I'm encouraged when they study the piece and discover with delight that it is not just another quilt but an expressive and compelling piece of fiber art.

I enjoy teaching workshops and giving lectures and trunk shows at different quilt venues. You may visit my blog, Life as a Quilter—Julia Graber (http://juliagraber.blogspot.com) to learn more about my life and quilting.

Inspiration and Design

I am challenged by taking an old familiar quilt block and turning it into something new and innovative with bright and bold colors. The New Quilts from an Old Favorite contest provides just that.

I enjoy using Electric Quilt 7 designing software to start the process and pick out the traditional block pattern and set it in different layouts, then rotate, color, and flip the block to make many samples. In the following two quilts I have set many different numbers of Flying Geese into an irregular grid:

I also tried the Carpenter's Wheel layout with different numbers of Flying Geese blocks inserted into that layout.:

I settled on this design and filled in the corners to complete my Twirly Birds.

Technique

I printed out each block of the Carpenter's Wheel layout and prepared each block for paper piecing. I only needed three different blocks but used fabrics in different colorways.

POURSUITE D'OIE SAUVAGE À PARIS (WILD GOOSE CHASE IN PARIS)

58" x 57"

Finalist
CHARLENE HEARST
Toronto, Ontario, Canada

Meet Charlene

Photo by Heike Blohm

I learned how to quilt during my gap year between high school and college/university. Quilting was something I always wanted to do but at the time seemed too difficult to teach myself from a library book. So I took a quilting course at our local library with my neighbor, who was also interested in learning how to quilt.

I was taught to quilt by an older lady using cardboard templates and scissors, sewing fabric pieces together by hand stitching, then quilting by hand. In the mid-1970s it was very hard to find 100-percent cotton fabric. At that time, we were using a polyester/cotton blend with either solid colors or calico prints. Quilt batting was polyester as well. Oh, how quilting tools and techniques have changed over the years! Belonging to a quilting guild and attending guild workshops have helped me develop my quilting skills over time.

As I worked full-time in a career in Parks and Recreation, quilting happened on the weekends. Sometimes it would take me a few years to finish a quilt. Now, being recently retired, I have days to sew and quilt, which is a luxury. So many ideas in my head! Now I have the time to transfer those ideas into quilts.

Recently I joined Instagram @charhearst and I am now being inspired by a whole new quilting community. Such a supportive and kind international community of quilters! I participated in their #100days100blocks challenge based on *Tula Pink's City Sampler: 100 Modern Blocks*. Through this experience I have "met" so many talented quilters. This is just the beginning of a new adventure in quilting and sharing of ideas.

Fabric and nature inspires my quilting. I love using the new, modern fabrics in my quilts combined with the simplicity of a modern quilt pattern. I like pieced patterns the best, and I love to incorporate stars and hearts fabrics and/or blocks into my quilts. My favorite shapes to piece are squares and triangles. I like all color combinations— neutrals, blues and greens, and more recently yellow! It is such a happy color! My family, friends, and colleagues are the recipients of my quilts.

I never really follow a quilt pattern. I like to create my own variation. I sew a test block first to see if I like the look of the pattern and the fabric combination before proceeding. I cut my fabric as I go, never cutting all at once, just in case I change my mind!

Quilting is my passion. I am at my happiest when I am sewing and creating quilts. When I am not in my sewing room (or as one family member likes to call it my "Quilt Cave"), I am enjoying life walking my dog, cycling, golfing, travelling, watching hockey, and taking photographs.

Inspiration and Design

Inspiration for my quilt came from the idea of a member of my quilting guild to form a small group of interested members to make quilts for the NQOF contest. A group of eight ladies (fellow finalist Katie Pidgeon among them) was interested and we had our first meeting in September 2015. We decided that each of us would create our own design for a quilt to enter in the contest. We met on seven occasions on Sunday afternoons to share ideas, show our progress, and give each other suggestions and feedback on our quilts.

We motivated and encouraged each other throughout the process and, surprisingly, all eight of our designs are completely different. Some of us finished our quilts and entered the contest, and others are still working on their quilts with the hope of finishing them in the next year. The great part is that we are continuing to meet as a group once a month.

I personally love the Flying Geese pattern, so I was quite excited to come up with an original design. I decided on my colors and fabrics first. I started with a monthly fat quarter bundle I had purchased in teals, off-white with black, and green. Next I went to my fabric stash and pulled more fabrics in these colors, as well as light grays that I thought would work well.

The design was inspired by the Paris map fabric from my stash and "a play on words" for the title—WILD GOOSE CHASE IN PARIS, or in French *Pursuite d'oie sauvage à Paris*. A member from our group had suggested titling the quilt first and taking inspiration from the title. What better way to show a wild goose chase then to create a maze through the streets of Paris! The Flying Geese blocks became the walls of the maze and the roads of Paris from the map fabric became the

pathway of the maze. This all came about when I was stitching one day with a member from our group.

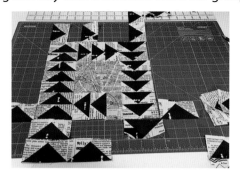

My inspiration for the "new quilts" aspect of the contest was to use the new, modern fabrics and trendy color combinations in a simple design with lots of negative space. Inspiration for the "old favorite" aspect of the contest was incorporating the traditional Flying Geese block into the design in a modern way. Another "old favorite" was to honor our past pioneer quilters by hand quilting the quilt, something I love to do and find very relaxing and soothing.

The biggest challenge I faced in making the quilt was that I did not have enough of the Paris map fabric to finish the quilt design. An online search began to find more of the map fabric. Luckily, I was able to find it locally in another colorway—an off-white and brown version. I would make it work. As you look at the quilt, you will notice that the outer edges of the maze pathways are in a different color from the center of the quilt.

After the quilt top was all finished, basted, and ready to hand quilt, guess what I found? The right colored map fabric! My dilemma: Do I buy the fabric and redo the quilt? Tempting, but too much work and not enough time left for me to hand quilt it in time if I did.

Technique

I tend to create quilts as I go and just start sewing. That is the approach I took with this quilt. Once I decided on the maze concept, I started to research possible maze layouts. I used graph paper to design the maze with two squares on the graph paper representing a finished 3" x 1½" Flying Geese block. Drawing the design on graph paper from the center out, I transferred the design to cutting the fabric. To keep track of where I was on my design as I was sewing, I would use pencil crayons and color in the areas completed on the graph paper.

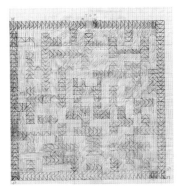

I started sewing my design from the center of the maze, cutting a 5" square (¼" seam allowance included) from the Paris map fabric. I chose to fussy-cut this piece as I wanted to highlight the center of the maze and the final destination as the *Jardin du Luxembourg* and *Palais du Luxembourg* (Luxembourg Garden and Palace).

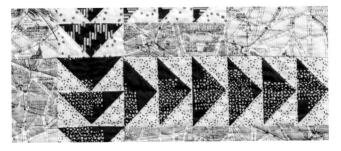

I began to build/sew the maze from this center square out. The walls of the maze are the Flying Geese blocks and the maze pathways are the Paris map fabric cut to size to form the rows between the Flying Geese blocks. The entrance to the maze is at the top of the quilt, and one follows the pathways to find the *Jardin du Luxembourg* in the center of the quilt.

I was originally going to make the Flying Geese blocks larger, but it was suggested by my group to make them smaller relative to the scale of the map. I sewed a test block first to make sure I had the right dimensions for the geese relative to the scale of the map fabric.

The Flying Geese block finished at 3" x 1½". To make each block, I used the traditional method with one 3½" x 2" rectangle in a teal green or green fabric for the body of the goose, and two 2" x 2" squares in an off-white with black or light gray fabric for the wings.

There are 385 Flying Geese blocks in the quilt.

Deciding on the backing fabric for the quilt was based on a fat quarter green print—the girls flying the kite and holding the pinwheels. I used leftover fabric from the backing to complete the outer border or wall of the maze. I fussy-cut the rectangles from this fabric.

The decision on the binding fabric was made after the quilt top was completed. I wanted to have some fun with the binding and I chose the irregular black stripe on off-white. I sewed the binding to the top side of the quilt by machine, then folded it over the edge of the quilt and sewed it in place by hand to the back of the quilt.

Quilting

The layers of the quilt were hand-basted before I hand quilted it. I used a natural color 100-percent glazed cotton thread to quilt along the roads of the map fabric and around the wings of the geese.

I used a variegated teal and brown Egyptian cotton 40-wt. thread to hand quilt through the center of the geese bodies. I was curious as to how many hours it would take me to hand quilt the quilt so I kept track of my hours. It took me a total of 96 hours over two months to complete the hand quilting. I did have a quilting buddy, my dog Cody, always by my side as I quilted.

FLY AWAY HOME 60" x 72"

Finalist

ANITA M. KARBAN-NEEF

Cary, Illinois

Meet Anita

Photo by Carolyn Ivancic

I've been quilting for about 20 years, though in the beginning it was only a small pieces. My interest really gained momentum around 2007 when I started taking on small quilting challenges and contests. From there, it spiraled in many different directions including full bed-size quilts, art quilts, and more contests and challenges.

I don't like to pigeon-hole my style, though I have found my quilt "voice" comes through most strongly when I am basing my design on traditional quilt designs, twisting them to be new and different, or with pictorial quilts. I like to call myself a TraditonalTwistArt Quilter. I find my work to be ever evolving.

Almost all commercial printed fabrics from my stash have been gifted away. As I favor working with batiks or hand-dyed fabrics, there is no sense in keeping fabric that can be better used by someone else. It also makes some room in the studio in my ongoing effort to simplify. It's amazing how quickly fabrics, quilting tools, and supplies accumulate on the cutting table. I need order in my space in order to create!

I've discovered that occasionally I need a break from original design work to remain fresh and creative. I admit I have a few (well, many) control issues. In an effort to counteract my overriding control, I occasionally participate in online quilt-alongs or mystery quilts. I still control colors and fabric but surrender design decisions. Sometimes you have to just let go and go with the flow. It adds another layer to the challenge.

My studio is the family room of our townhouse and also doubles as my work-from-home office. Since it's not a large room, it's in an ever-changing state of reorganization. I found a rolling computer desk that houses my docking station and two computer monitors, placed in an L configuration that allows the electronics to share a power source strip with whichever sewing machine I'm using. My husband gifted me a new leather executive office chair, which has made a world of difference in my comfort whether I'm working or sewing.

Quilting is my time to be with my thoughts while my hands are kept busy, so I don't currently belong to any local guilds. In the age of instant communication, I use my quilt blog (www.cherryquilt.blogspot.com) to share my quilting adventures and keep in touch with fellow quilt bloggers across the globe. This year I have plans to attend QuiltWeek® – Paducah and a few other quilt shows.

My current job requires some travel, which usually involves me squeezing in some quilt fabric shopping whenever I can. On a trip to Switzerland, I was able to purchase some of their beautiful, world-renowned embroidered fabrics. These may just be showing up in a future quilt design!

I am extremely lucky to have a very supportive husband, Wil, encouraging my quilt work. Most of all, he understands my need to create, which sometimes overrides everything else in our lives. He patiently waits, knowing that balance will eventually come round again.

The very first planning I did for the New Quilts from an Old Favorite: Flying Geese was to purchase a selection of bright, citrusy batiks and the dark blue for the background when I visited the AQS show back in April of 2015.

Citrus batiks

I sketched out several free-flowing, loopy trailing designs in a notebook, which promptly ended up gathering dust in the dark recesses of a cabinet. It didn't feel right and the design was not inspiring me at all. The batiks I chose were too self-limiting. After all, I have an extensive collection of batiks in my stash (around 740, give or take, not counting precuts, light neutrals, recent additions, etc.) and here I was trying to only use 11. It's no wonder the design wasn't going anywhere anytime soon!

Fast forward to summer of 2016, and the time had come to get busy designing and stitching on this project.

Several years ago, the thought of making Flying Geese intimidated me. Triangles of any kind are tricky and I wasn't going anywhere near them. Then along came the small quilt I designed for another competition combining Flying Geese with Bird in the Air blocks. The result was MIDNIGHT FLIGHT TO THE FOUR WINDS. Making this little quilt got me over my

MIDNIGHT FLIGHT TO THE FOUR WINDS, made by Anita, 28" x 28"

fear of wrestling with triangles. And I learned there were many different ways to make Flying Geese; I just needed to find the way that worked for me to get the result I wanted.

Ever since then, I always wanted to make an expanded version of the design. The original version always looked confined—kind of cut off before it could really play out to a dynamic design. This was the direction I needed to go for the NQOF contest. Things really started coming together once I got out of my own way. I still had my original graph paper drawings so I could focus on expanding the Bird in the Air block to suit my new design, as well as flipping the direction of the Flying Geese to maintain the outward motion of the quilt, building out larger wing spans.

I started out simple with a repeat of the rounds and a few variations of that layout, but thought them too plain, too symmetrical, too boring. I played around with an offset Barn Raising setting, which played well with the color progression I had in mind. All the blocks and Flying Geese runs were designed on a 1" block grid.

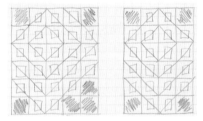

Once I figured out the design blocks and layout, I need to determine the color progression and narrow down the fabric choices.

I went from the original 11 batiks to using 64 different batiks in the final design! The expanded fabric range added so much more depth to the design. Once I had the colors sorted out, I cut all the pieces for the Bird blocks first, along with the blue background.

Three colors cut

Blue pieces

For accuracy's sake, I chose to make the sub-units using the stitch-and-flip corner method with squares and rectangles. This method does require extra yardage, as there is some extra waste. I reordered the background blue twice and ended up with only a 14" square left over. That was cutting it too close for comfort!

Each Bird requires 38 separate pieces, all sewn in a specific order. It's easier to handle this by sewing all the possible smaller sub-units first. To help with keeping track of the bird pieces, I made a color-coded cutting sheet. The finished Bird blocks were done in four color families, shaded from light to dark, with the progression moving out from the center in rounds.

Once the Bird blocks were complete, it was time to move on to constructing all the Flying Geese runs. My batik stash was missing a few clear shades of some of the cooler colors, necessitating a quick shopping to fill out the color ranges.

The one drawback to the design for FLY AWAY HOME was that I did not have a full color plan to follow. Instead, I worked from a taped and glued together black-and-white graph paper diagram. Never again! It would have been helpful to have a color plan when I decided to reverse the Flying Geese run direction and when working out the wing tip intersection. Instead, I ended up sketching out a few different junction ideas separately rather then redoing the entire plan.

The quilt was assembled from the center out in sections, rather than rows. This way I was able to deal with the tricky wing connections and block spacer rows.

The Barn Raising setting of the Bird blocks, which are outlined by the Flying Geese runs, echo larger imagined Flying Geese runs.

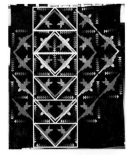

All of the quilting was done on a domestic sewing machine, a Singer® Scholastic 6510. Its greatest feature is the auto tension, allowing me to put almost anything under the needle. Here is a photo of the quilting underway.

I outlined the bird shapes and larger rectangles sections in blue before moving on to the detail quilting of each bird in the appropriate color. The bird quilting was not marked out in full lines, just with a small dot/slash to aim toward. For the blue background, I marked lines lightly in silver pencil.

I chose not to fill the entire quilt top with pieced blocks. On the large solid blue areas, I quilted the outline of the Bird in the Air design, creating "ghost" birds flying on ahead of the flock. To achieve some semblance of accuracy, I traced an actual Bird block and cut a lightweight cardboard stencil to draw around to mark the quilting lines.

FLY AWAY HOME has a total of 364 Flying Geese. I think there will be another rendition of this quilt in the future—not sure when, but there are a few things I want to explore in another direction, letting the Flying Geese lead the way.

SILLY GOOSE 50½" x 59"

Finalist
CHRIS LYNN KIRSCH
Watertown, Wisconsin

Meet Chris

Photo by Michael Kirsch

I began quilting in 1987 when my sister-in-law talked me into taking a class. She never finished her first quilt, but I became addicted! I had a husband and children to care for and a part-time job as a dental hygienist. My life seemed full, but it was about to become much fuller. I HAD TO QUILT! I made time for it whenever I could squeeze in a moment. I never imagined quilting would become such a big part of my life.

My two favorite subjects in school were geometry and home economics (mostly the sewing part). I guess I was destined to quilt. I began with very traditional pieced patterns. With time, I wanted to try things I couldn't find patterns for, but with no background in art I didn't think I could do it. Friends encouraged me to try making the projects in my mind, and the first time I did my quilt won an award! It was just the beginning. Now I make both traditional and art quilts. I love it all, and I'm very grateful for my sewing background because it gave me the tools to put into cloth the projects filling my brain.

I make quilts because I can't stop. The ideas just seem to come to me and I simply must try and see if I can make them happen. I enjoy the problem solving involved in creating an original piece of fiber art. I love helping others find the creativity inside themselves even more. I've also discovered I enjoy dissecting and putting into words the how-tos of what I do, so writing patterns and eventually books was a natural progression for me (*Snuggle and Learn Quilts for Kids*, Martingale and Co., 2008).

Currently, I collect quilts, design quilts, teach others how to make quilts, enter quilts in competitions, write books about making quilts, and take groups of quilters on cruises/tours in the United States and Europe. I even have a weekly blog in which I share many of my techniques and experiences. You may join in on my blog at: http://chrisquilts.net/blog. This certainly wasn't what I expected to be doing in life, but I'm learning never to say never when it comes to quilting.

Artists are inspired by many things and my faith in Jesus Christ is a huge part of my inspiration. He has given me the abilities and opportunities to do what I love, and my hope is that my work brings Him glory.

I've come to an interesting point in my life. My husband and I watch our grandchildren (ages five and two) full-time while Mommy and Daddy are at work. When I decided this was something I wanted to do, I thought my quilting life would be put on the back burner. But, with the encouragement of my wonderful husband of 40 years, I am able to continue to quilt while raising a new generation of kids. What a blessing, because, as I said before, I have to quilt!

Inspiration and Design

SILLY GOOSE was inspired by The National Quilt Museum contest and my love of wordplay. While in Paducah during QuiltWeek® 2016, I started contemplating what I could do with the Flying Geese pattern. Quilting is the fun part of my life, and I try to show that joy in each piece I create. I began running "goose" expressions through my mind, and when I hit on "silly goose" it all started to come together. To portray a silly goose, one would need other, non-silly geese.

To give the illusion of depth, a gradation of color would work well. This led me to the Cherrywood fabric booth at the Rotary Club (one of my favorite QuiltWeek stops). Now that I had the fabric and the idea, I couldn't wait to get home and begin.

I recently made a quilt using metallic spandex and wool batting. The stretchiness of the fabric gave a faux trapunto look, and the shininess gave the quilt a wonderful shimmer. I wanted to use it again to make the silly goose stand out from the rest! I came up with a paisley design, purchased some brightly colored metallic fabrics, and machine appliquéd the paisleys using my Reverse Repliqué technique. It worked! She definitely makes a statement.

Working with the sticky/stretchy fabric did present a few challenges, but I persevered and feel it was worth it. (See page 71 for information on my technique.)

The background quilting took a bit of brainstorming. I wanted it to add to the solo goose's "silliness" and felt I could achieve this with swirls of trapunto floating in her wake. To make these swirls stand out, I chose to free-motion embroider the interior of many of the swirls prior to layering the quilt sandwich. In this way, the embroidery would "pop," creating the effect I was looking for. The strategically placed heat-set crystals were the icing on the cake.

Now what to do in the rest of the sky? More lines of obedient geese seemed the best answer. Once they were quilted, I chose stippling and spirals to fill in the rest, because those are the designs I most like to stitch.

I certainly had my "what next?" and "oh no!" moments while making this quilt, but every time I look at it, it makes me smile. The description on my label says it all: "There's one in every crowd. She can't seem to follow the leader or the rules. What a silly goose!"

Technique: Reverse Repliqué - Working with Shiny, Stretchy Fabric

A few years ago I saw a machine-quilted sample in a vendor booth at a quilt show that blew me away. The sample sandwich had a cotton backing, wool batting, and the top was a metallic spandex. Some areas of the sample were quilted heavily, others were left unquilted, and the stretchy fabric poofed up in the unquilted areas as if they were trapunto, while the light danced off the shiny fabric. I knew I was destined to try it. On that same trip, I happened into a fabric store that had a piece of a beautiful copper color spandex fabric on the clearance rack. Two yards of it came home with me, and a few months later I took a guild challenge to make an Art Deco-themed quilt. I came up with a geometric design, added a black cotton fabric to the palette, and began using my Repliqué technique to create a quilt I named FORTY WONDERFUL YEARS (in honor of my husband and my fortieth wedding anniversary).

FORTY WONDERFUL YEARS

It was quite a challenge to work with this non-traditional fabric, but the effects were exactly what I was looking for. When I began working on SILLY GOOSE, I felt it was time to revisit this technique to make the title goose stand out.

It was fun shopping for the different stretchy fabrics, and, when I couldn't find the right orange, I chose to add polar fleece to the mix. I think the fuzzy texture worked in this project.

Because the paisleys were made from a number of different stretchy fabrics, I chose to make them using a technique I call Reverse Repliqué that places the satin stitching on the cotton fabric giving a lovely, finished look. Satin stitching on the stretchy fabric would have been more of a challenge, and it wouldn't have finished as smoothly.

Once the paisleys were complete, I appliquéd the silly goose to the background. By layering my quilt

with two batts—a wool batt on top of a cotton batt—quilting around each paisley on the outside of the satin stitching, and then quilting heavily in the background, the trapunto effect was complete.

Reverse Repliqué

1. Draw a paisley (or any shape) in place on the right side of the base fabric with a removable marker. I prefer a sliver of soap.

2. Place an oversized piece of the "paisley" fabric underneath the base fabric, right side of paisley fabric to wrong side of base fabric, being sure it covers the entire drawn shape. Pin around the edges.

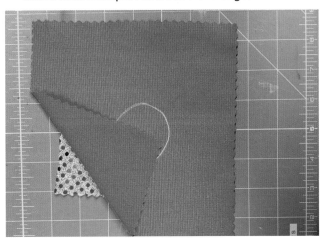

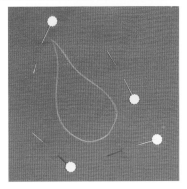

3. On the top side, in a thread to match the base fabric, stitch around the shape on the marked line.

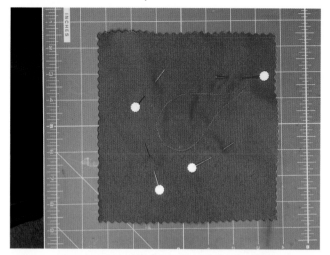

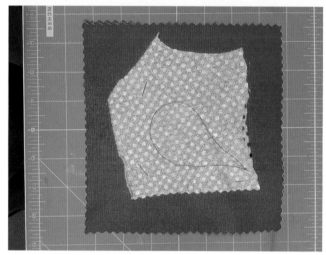

4. Carefully trim the base fabric away from the shape close to the stitching.

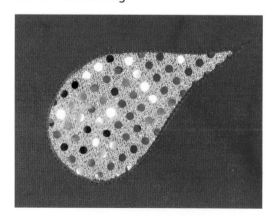

5. Place a piece of stabilizer behind the area to be machine appliquéd and satin stitch around the shape, covering both the raw edge of the base fabric and the straight stitching in step 3. HINT: To prevent the toe of the presser foot from sticking to the stretchy fabric, place a small piece of paper between the foot and the fabric, moving it along as needed.

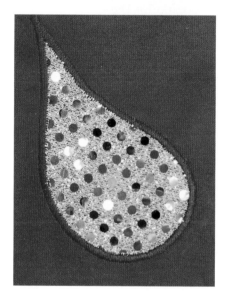

6. Repeat for all the shapes. Trim the excess fabric away from behind each shape.

GLAD PLAID GOOSE DANCE 59" x 59"

Finalist
ANN L. PETERSEN
Surprise, Arizona

Meet Ann

Photo by Bonnie McCaffery

Quilting and sewing are family traditions and I learned much about both from my mom and grandmothers. Their work has always been inspirational. But I was mostly a crafter and garment sewer with an occasional quilt from a pattern thrown in until well into the mid-1990s.

Then one day, with a little more than an hour to spare before my son returned from school, I passed a street banner advertising a quilt show. On a whim, I turned into the lot and went to see the Arapahoe County Quilters Festival of Quilts. I fell in love. I have always loved geometric quilting patterns and color and fabric, but these quilts were so dynamic! With such wonderful colors and intricate patterns and creative energy, I knew I would work from that moment on to learn how to make quilts like that.

It has been slow work to learn how to foster my own creativity, but I believe it is a skill someone can learn and practice and improve. I began to take quilt classes from both local and national quilters. Then I started to work at my local quilt shop and found more inspiration from customers and fellow employees. I joined the Arapahoe County Quilters, and I'm so grateful for the opportunities and friendship I found there. (I was far too shy to join after I saw the first show, but I really wish that I had. It took a year of working at the shop and feeling comfortable with more of the quilting community before I dared to join. That was too bad.)

The rich and varied community of quilters gives me a welcome as well as constant inspiration, all of which have allowed me to create. And there is little more rewarding than those creative moments.

My small successes in the quilt world have enabled me to travel and teach others some of my techniques. I also get to teach online classes on Craftsy and thoroughly enjoy that as well. Showing others ways to improve their skills is delightful, and I just hope an occasional student finds as much fulfillment in this art as I have.

GLAD PLAID GOOSE DANCE was specifically designed for this contest. I started with a collection of bright woven plaids that I have been buying for years. Because these fabrics play well with

bright batiks, I selected two colorways of each type of fabric. The colors I liked the best were warm versus cool colors. A range of reds to yellows versus teals to purples in each group were pulled and piled on my sewing table.

Next, I started designing several New York Beauty-style blocks, each incorporating Flying Geese variations. I printed these onto freezer paper and made three blocks.

I thought I would play on the design wall and see where that led. I had been playing with layouts in Electric Quilt® software, including this one with Winding Ways blocks. Subbing in the NYB blocks for the Winding Ways really didn't work. So I tried several more—diagonals? chevrons?—but nothing seemed to inspire me.

I went back to Electric Quilt and decided to make one large block. Trying it as the center of an asymmetrical medallion did catch my interest, so I made it up. Once complete, I realized it needed to be bigger so I designed another round of geese around the outside edge and sewed that onto the center. This was pieced into a large plaid piece of fabric, another favorite technique.

Adding borders of different widths to offset the medallion was my next task. From this point on, I would finish a step, decide what kind of border the quilt was asking me to make, design the border in EQ, and sew it. Each border design was only for two sides and all

were different widths until I reached the outer edge. I wanted the second border to be wider on the lower and right sides, and the New York Beauty blocks I had already constructed seemed to work well, so I designed more blocks using Flying Geese and then made a two-side border with them.

I found this step-by-step method using EQ to work well for me. I love to paper piece and designing blocks in EQ and printing them on freezer paper is an easy and wonderful technique for creating blocks in any size the quilt may need. However, I have decided that designing a whole quilt in the software can be frustrating. I often can sew something that is well beyond either my capabilities in EQ or beyond the capabilities of the software. I also find that it takes away much of the joy of creating a quilt to draw it digitally and then simply follow the pattern.

The interplay between my slowly growing quilt and sparks of inspiration based on what I see on the wall is what drives me to create quilts. Many artists speak of the work talking to them or feeling divine inspiration. I know the feeling well and find those moments to be ones of pure joy. Designing on the wall with real fabric and only using the computer for making block patterns that I am envisioning is the best method for me.

In the end I had a computer design for the entire quilt, but that digital image came from the actual quilt as I sewed. This wouldn't always be possible, because there are setting techniques I can't replicate with software; but this method worked with the medallion design.

Techniques

Without a doubt, my favorite technique for making a quilt top is paper piecing using freezer paper. This method allows me to use very few paper patterns, instead of one for each block, as the freezer paper is used over and over for many blocks. With this technique, you press

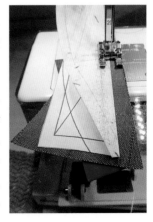

the plastic side of the paper to the fabric, fold the paper on the stitching lines, and sew next to the fold instead of stitching through the paper. So at the end of the block you simply peel off the paper instead of ripping tiny pieces of paper from underneath the stitches.

I also cut templates for each piece of a block from the freezer paper. Each template is the finished size of the piece in the block, and I can then press it to fabric and cut it about ⅜" – ½" larger all around. I want the angles to be correct and fabric piece to be bigger than needed—always a good strategy when paper piecing.

When I have more than one block to do, I will make two copies of my pattern and use them to do a modified version of chain piecing. I will sew pieces 1 & 2 together on one block, and then, without cutting the thread, sew pieces 1 & 2 together on the second block. Then I can snip the first block from the second and add piece 3 to the first block; snip the second block free and add piece 3 to it. Using only two patterns, I can chain piece many blocks two at a time. This saves time and thread.

Paper piecing allows me to easily design a block in the computer and then print it out at whatever size I wish. It can be a very freeing way to design.

I quilt all my quilts (whatever their size) on my domestic machine, a BERNINA 550. The geometric design and amazing colors available to me are wonderful, but the sculptural element, which brings the piece to life, is the quilting. This quilt was done with many straight line quilting designs, to either reflect the plaids or enhance them. I practice my quilting before actually stitching on my quilt so that I am sure about my design.

Sometimes I followed the lines of the plaid to quilt, adding a dense stipple to give the plaid dimension; other times I quilted a plaid over a batik area. Two other filler designs were based on straight lines. One I call *corduroy* quilting because it is straight lines; but since they are mostly quilted free motion, the occasional (or sometimes frequent) wobbles give the quilting the look of corduroy where the lines (or wales) tend to be brushed one way or another. The other has shorter lines connected with a curved end done in a checkerboard

pattern. I deliberately avoided curvaceous quilting like feathers or cables to more strongly emphasize the woven plaid fabrics.

When it was time to add the binding, I chose two of my favorite plaid fabrics but still felt that the quilt wanted another detail. I often add piping to binding because it gives a lovely crisp edge to the quilt. I use Susan Cleveland's Piping Hot Binding tool and book for this technique (piecesbewithyou.com). As I was sewing my piping, I wondered what adding a decorative stitch to it would look like. So I experimented a little and found I liked a simple blind hemstitch with a hand-dyed variegated perle cotton from Laura Wasilowski (artfabrik. com) that I found in my stash.

One thing always leads to another, and I felt the quilt needed some of this variegated thread in the center as well. So I added some ellipses in the center and outlined the center circle with thread using hand embroidery.

Finalist
KATIE PIDGEON
Toronto, Ontario, Canada

Meet Katie

Photo by Arthur Pidgeon

I didn't learn to quilt from a grandmother, aunt, or mother. In primary school, my mom signed me up for a stitchery class and I have loved anything with a needle since. Quilting was something I was never exposed to as a child. We didn't have quilts on our beds or have quilts that had been passed down from generation to generation. My educational background was not in the fine art realm, so, again I was not exposed to the world of fiber art and artistic creativity.

It wasn't until the year 2000 that I discovered quilting. I used to go to a few quilt stores and would dabble with some fabrics a little. I even bought a quilting pattern of a Mariner's Compass and just started sewing it together. I didn't know anything, so that quilt has no mistakes in it. Even though it was made with polyester fabric and probably polyester batting and doesn't quite lie flat in some centers of the compass, I loved it. I loved the process of making it, with a combination of machine sewing and hand quilting. I hung that quilt on my dining room wall for years. Even then, I didn't associate a quilt with having to only be on a bed.

I joined a local guild and started taking the workshops that they offered each year. From hand appliqué, to fusing, machine quilting, and pictorials, I wanted to learn as much as possible. With the different techniques, different teaching methods, tools, fabrics, and threads, I have learned lots over the years. I have learned what I love and what I will never do again, and sometimes I even finish a workshop project.

Quilting usually happens in the evening as my "down time" after a hectic day. I'm able to block out the world and just relax. Because of this, I especially love hand appliqué and hand quilting. This is done at a slow speed that allows my mind to wander. I may be thinking about the next stitch, the next piece that will be appliquéd, or how I may quilt the finished top. I enjoy going into my quilting room and either starting on a project or just puttering around, pulling out fabrics and seeing what catches my fancy.

Quilting has also expanded my circle of friends. It has opened a whole new world of sharing creative ideas and of going to different places to see quilts, take workshops, and buy fabric. My nine-to-five job is in the financial sector, which is not the most creative place to be, so quilting allows me to stretch my creative muscles.

Some of my inspiration comes from participating in guild challenges. Other inspiration just happens. Sometimes I might be practicing a certain technique or learning a new embroidery stitch; and from that little start, a quilt may be the outcome. I don't use patterns as I don't find that inspiring, since it is not my idea. Sometimes a little doodle will spark a finished quilt.

Inspiration and Design

In 2015, I saw the New Quilts from an Old Favorite: New York Beauty exhibit at AQS QuiltWeek® in Syracuse, New York, and was totally blown away with the variety possible from one simple block. I returned home to Canada still intrigued with the quilts that I saw and decided that I needed to do the challenge myself. I put an announcement in my guild's newsletter to see if others would be interested. Eight of us formed a group in the fall of 2015, including Charlene Hearst, a fellow finalist.

When I saw that the block pattern for 2017 was the Flying Geese block, I thought, "Well, this is fantastic," as I had recently taken a Flying Geese class from Gail Garber (another finalist) and wanted to make use of what I had learned. What perfect timing; I just knew this was meant to be.

We met once a month and decided that at each meeting we would have a specific phase done on our quilts. For instance, at the first meeting, we talked about the competition and what it meant to us. For the next meeting, the goal was to have a design idea, then a color scheme, and slowly each quilt started forming. When we met, we would discuss design ideas, color combinations, technical and quilting challenges, and how the quilting would be done.

We were amazed by how many different ideas came from a simple block pattern. The group provided deadlines and momentum to keep us going on our individual projects.

The first thing I had to work on was the finished size of the quilt. 50" x 50" is pretty big for a challenge, and I didn't want to finish the quilt to find that it wasn't the right size. I started by taping paper together to the finished size to see how big 50" x 50" is, which is pretty big, and added a few inches to be on the safe side.

The design idea just happened. I liked the idea of the spokes coming out of a central point. I felt it would emphasize the "flying" part of the block name. Each spoke would be a variation of the Flying Geese pattern with appliqué motifs wrapped around each spoke.

When I'm working on a challenge, I find that the overall design concept comes pretty quickly. Either the theme or what I want to do with the quilt afterwards helps formulate what I produce.

Picking the colors, on the other hand, is something completely different. Over the years, I have taken various color theory classes. In 2012 while in Houston, I took a class with Weeks Ringle about picking a picture you liked and pulling out the different colors, values, and proportions from it. In 2014, our guild hosted a local quilter, Heather Stewart, who also talked about color theory and pulling colors from a picture to determine your color palette for your quilt. For this quilt, that is exactly what I did.

The colors I choose came from a picture of a 1950-style Ferris wheel. I took the picture to Home Depot and picked out the colors in the picture using paint chips. Then I matched the paint chips to my stash and only used fabrics that corresponded to the paint chips.

The title of my piece Lucy Goosy @ the Improv came pretty much when I had finished the overall design and size of my quilt. The "Lucy Goosy" part is definitely from the block name. The "Improv" is a reference to the fact that I didn't know what the finished quilt was going to look like. I would pull out colors when working on a section; and when that section was finished, I would move onto the next section, with another set of colors pulled.

Technique

With a quilt block called Flying Geese, I wanted to give my quilt the feeling of being carefree. I didn't want a plain background, but I did want the background to stay in the background.

The quilt is made up of 10 spokes radiating out of the center. In order to incorporate hand appliqué into my piece, I divided the quilt design into separate triangular sections. With three different off-white fabrics picked, I used 2" x 2" and 4" x 4" squares to create the background, one size square per section, sewing them together in no particular color order. Each Flying Geese spoke is paper foundation pieced, which meant hours of tearing out tiny paper pieces. The spokes are all different variations of the Flying Geese block, and each spoke is completely different in shape, direction, and pattern.

As each section took shape, I would start appliquéing. The side of one section would have the paper foundation Flying Geese hand sewn on, and once the next section was completed, it would be sewn onto

the other side of the spoke. As I finished each section with this technique, the full quilt started to take shape.

When I was starting on an individual section, I knew what the appliqué motifs would be and that they would be mirrored on the opposite spoke to keep a sense of balance. My sketch of the design was never more than a pencil drawing, so I had no overall idea of where the colors would be or what the combinations would show. From the colors that I had set aside to use for this quilt based on my Ferris Wheel picture, I would pull out the number of fabrics needed for a specific spoke and start from there. The appliqué motifs are all drawn freely—I just played with a pencil and paper and doodled.

I used needle-turn appliqué with freezer-paper templates and a 60/2 cotton thread, which blends nicely into both the background and the main appliqué fabric.

As I completed each section, I used 8-wt. pearle cotton to hand embroider some additional details into some of the sections.

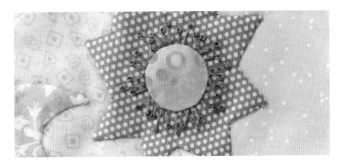

When it came time to put the quilt together, I used a Warm & White cotton batting. Using a 100-percent cotton thread, I hand quilted it using an echo pattern. To further enhance the feeling of carefree flight in my piece, I hand quilted Flying Geese spokes into the background sections in off-white 8-wt. pearle cotton.

CHILLY GOOSE, NO FEATHERS

52½" x 53½"

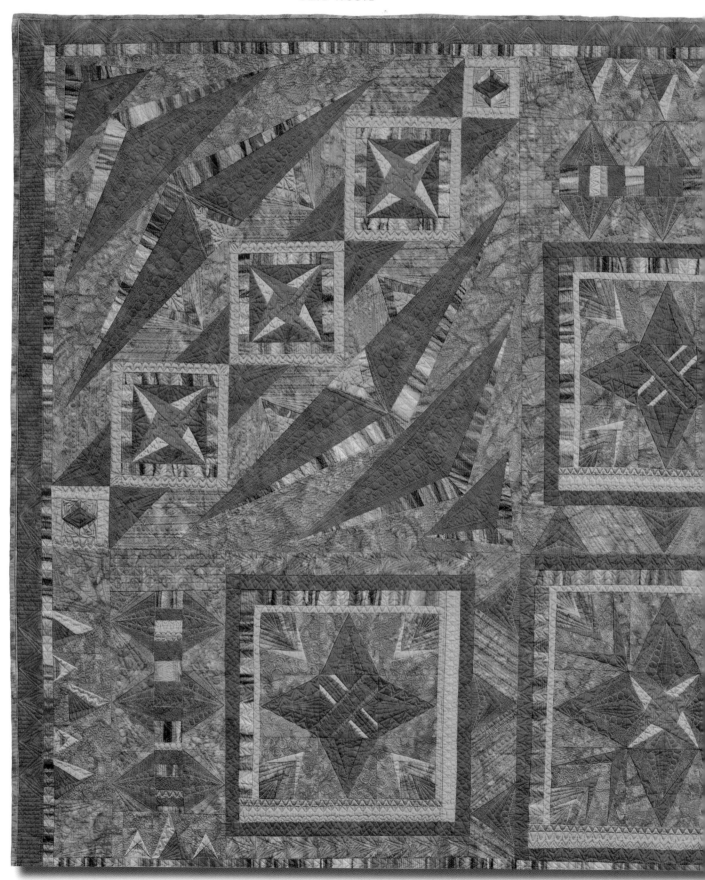

Finalist
ALICIA STERNA
Surprise, Arizona

Meet Alicia

Photo by Randy Sterna

For six summers, my husband and I volunteered for the Forest Service at Cape Perpetua, a scenic area on the coast of Oregon near a little town called Yachats. One summer in the early 2000s while driving our 30-foot Airstream trailer to our summer assignment, we stopped in at a colorful quilt shop in Roseburg, Oregon. The staff began convincing me I needed to take up quilting. I was not an easy sell, but they were persistent and despite the fact I had no machine and was living in my trailer for the next five months, they convinced me that it was all possible. Within two days I had bought a machine, the tools of the trade, fabric, and an instruction book. Two weeks later, I had completed two placemats.

Over the next few years I watched quilting shows and bought books and magazines, both of which helped me improve by skills. I took my first quilting class about five years after I began quilting. I have always quilted my own pieces and rarely use patterns. However, lack of formal training and independence does result in many challenges. Every quilt includes a Plan B for when my original plan does not work. This quilt was no different, but each time some issue is resolved, I feel great satisfaction.

I have taught classes on expanding creativity to my local quilting club and that not only helped other quilters think differently about their options for quilting, but also pushed me to try many different techniques and materials and incorporate them into my quilts.

After a career as a lawyer for the state police organization in Arizona and the manager of the state risk management program where I worked mostly with ideas and managed paper, quilting provides me with tangible work products, an opportunity for endless creativity, and a sense of artistry.

"It's Only Fabric" and "Too Many Choices Inhibit Creativity" are two maxims I live by. There is nothing wrong with fabric collecting, but if you are a quilter, you really have to cut fabric up and use it. There is always more. When undecided what to do next, the overwhelming and endless selection of fabric and patterns can result in an inability to make a decision and move ahead. Participating in challenges allows me to channel and limit my choices so I can move forward.

I am a finisher and tend to work on only one large piece at a time. Often, there is a second, small project I am working on that travels easily to my weekly quilting bee. The relationships built with those quilters and others in my quilting community are of utmost importance in my life. My husband is a very supportive self-titled "Quilt Consultant." He happily travels to shows around the country and has furnished a quilting studio not only in our home but also in a shed built next to our Airstream trailer, which is currently set up as a cabin in the mountains of Arizona and is where we spend our summers. I surely have what I need to create. Now it is up to me to continue to do so.

I am already working on designs for the 2018 NQOF Bow Tie challenge.

Inspiration and Design

I like challenges. They provide parameters to help with design, timeframes to keep me focused, and an opportunity to do something new. This is my first entry into New Quilts from an Old Favorite contest. Although I have made many bed quilts, my work mostly features art quilt techniques and contemporary designs. However, I usually include altered traditional block patterns in my designs.

A stroll after breakfast at a new restaurant brought me by some high-end clothing shops. A black-and-white striped dress, with bold blocks of solid color randomly inserted in the stripes, inspired the original idea for this quilt. The design evolved quickly but in no way resembles the dress. I, too, selected bold colors and the solid color blocks placed on the dress informed the design of the unequally sized large Star blocks and irregular placement of the blocks in the final quilt. No black or white made it into the quilt.

My husband had given me EQ7 software last spring, and although not particularly computer savvy, I was determined to use the program to expand design options for my quilts. Six weeks of working on tutorials and altering

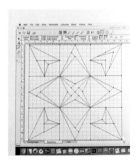

standard block patterns in the program made me comfortable enough to design original blocks.

I discovered I could make blocks of various sizes with numerous parts. The larger blocks are based on the Nine Patch block. The program makes templates for cutting fabric for my blocks and patterns for paper piecing were printable. With no final plan of how to use them, I began making blocks. I had decided not to include traditional Flying Geese in the quilt early on in the design, but instead I included a number of variations on the theme. I researched to find various interpretations of Flying Geese blocks. The most traditional Flying Geese blocks in my quilt are found in the background.

Often when working on quilts, I limit my fabric choice to my stash. Fabric selection was based on a desire to make what I call Shadow Flying Geese blocks using two batik teals from my stash, and to use fat quarters of five bright Robert Kaufman Radiance silks. They were purchased four years prior and those same colors were no longer available, so my design and the colors used were limited by the supply on hand. The multicolored batik was the one new fabric I purchased.

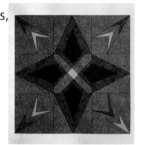

I tried several iterations of block placement on my design wall. The final placement was determined after adding the large Flying Geese to the sides of the row of three smaller pink-centered blocks. Some completed blocks and runs of Flying Geese never made it into the final design.

Inspiration is everywhere and I find hiking and walking to be especially creative times. Museums of all types provide pattern, color, and design ideas. I have a dedicated quilting space, and being retired allows me to happily work whenever I choose. I am most creative early in the day, so I rarely quilt at night. I do not thrive under pressure and tend to finish pieces well before any deadline. I intend to continue to explore EQ7 for use in my designs.

Technique

The three large Star blocks, composed of my Shadow Flying Geese, were designed and pieced first. I used the freezer-paper method of paper piecing I learned from my friend Ann Petersen, also a finalist in this contest. The precision at the star points was great, but the lump produced under the points by so many layers of fabric meeting at that one point provided quite the quilting challenge later.

Then came various Flying Geese sections in a variety of shapes and sizes. The design wall was crucial in determining the final layout. Many different design options were pinned to the wall, photos were taken, and the layout was considered over several weeks as additional sections of the quilt were pieced and additional fabrics auditioned for use. Pieced borders for the large blocks never made it into the quilt. Sections combining Flying Geese with colorful blocks of fabric also proved unacceptable. Sometimes a design was rejected due to problems anticipated with putting it together; other times, it just did not give the look desired. Symmetry was important, but repetition was not my goal.

Construction proved easier once I decided to make the various parts fit into four large blocks that were sewn together in the final layout. Filling in the spaces of these four large blocks was challenging, as the spaces were not just on the outside edges but sprinkled throughout the large quilt block.

I placed the parts making up the larger blocks on my cutting mat to help determine exact size of pieces I needed to add. I then tried various fabrics and patterns

but options were limited by the amount of silk fabric left. I used just about every square inch of it. Completing these four large blocks took more time than any other part of the construction.

I photographed the finished top and only then noticed that one of the Star Point blocks in the lower left large Star block was turned in the wrong direction! That block was removed, turned, and sewn back in place. That is the only hand stitching on this quilt.

I sketched many quilting designs before starting the quilting. I drew designs directly onto Glad® Press'n Seal® Wrap and placed it on the quilt to see if each design really worked as intended. I do not like to heavily mark my quilts, but did use white pencil markings on some areas. I used blue painter's tape to avoid marking the silks.

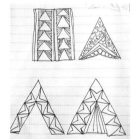

Colored quilting threads emphasized certain areas and added parallelograms that I could then quilt with lines and a variety of fills. I often had to take out and redo the quilting when what I thought would work just did not produce the desired effect. As with the piecing, I wanted lots of variations on the Flying Geese theme in my quilting.

I completed the quilting on my domestic machine. This step is often the most fun for me. Early on, I decided I would use no feather designs and that decision inspired the name of the quilt. The quilting took almost as long to complete as the piecing.

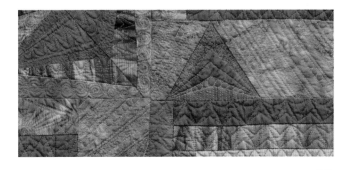

Finalist
SUE TURNQUIST
Tifton, Georgia

Meet Sue

Photo by Kenneth West

As I approach my "golden years" (not exactly sure what those are, but I'm almost 60), I pause to remember my journey through the competitive quilting world. The National Quilt Museum's New Quilts from an Old Favorite competition has been a favorite of mine for many years. I didn't discover the contest until 1998 when I made my first, starry-eyed visit to the museum and viewed the exhibit of Pineapple quilts from the 1998 contest. I wanted to see one of my quilts hanging in that prestigious gallery

My very first entry was in 1997 when the Old Favorite was the Kaleidoscope block. I was shocked that my quilt was a finalist and I floated on air when I saw it hanging in the museum. My second entry, in the Storm at Sea competition in 2000, was honored to receive a second-place ribbon. I will always remember crossing the stage at the AQS awards ceremony in the old Expo auditorium to receive my prize. Shortly thereafter, my name was announced as the third-place winner in the AQS Wall Quilt category. I didn't sleep that night. What a banner year that was. I was hooked on competitive quilting.

I was fortunate to have quilts accepted in the Feathered Star and Monkey Wrench competitions in

2003 and 2004, respectively. Every year that I had a finalist quilt in the contest, I made a beeline for the museum as soon as I arrived in Paducah for QuiltWeek. The thrill of having a quilt hanging in the museum never goes away. Then came a long hiatus away from quilting as I switched careers and gradually assumed more and more caregiving responsibilities for my aging mother. Mom passed away in 2009 and another career change followed in 2011.

After beginning a new job and settling into a new community, I polished up my rusty quilting skills and my Basket quilt became a finalist in 2012. My Carolina Lily and Nine Patch entries were finalists in 2013 and 2014, respectively. Last year (2016) my beloved zebra quilt (Do These Stripes Make My Butt Look Big?) placed first in the New York Beauty challenge and I was thrilled. That elation was short-lived when the zebra was not selected to grace the book cover.

The thrill of acceptance has never diminished, however, and I was honored to have Farm Alarm accepted for the current year.

The talented folks who enter this contest, as well as the regional and national shows, continue to inspire me and drive me to more creative endeavors. Ladies in the quilting world are incredibly giving of themselves and I am grateful for the friendships I've made over the years. I am equally grateful for the friends I've made in local quilt guilds. Always humble, these ladies and gentlemen don't have any idea how creative and talented they really are and how much I depend on them to inspire me.

Now, mostly retired and enjoying my free time to create, I am continuously learning new skills that enable my quilts to come alive.

Inspiration and Design/Techniques

As an animal science major at Arkansas State University, I was taken under the wing of one of the professors who was in charge of the university poultry farm. I had raised chickens while growing up in rural Arkansas, and Dr. James Keene hired me to work at the university's layer chicken farm. This was back in the 1970s when there weren't very many women in agricultural fields. I was the first female he had ever hired.

It wasn't long before I was offered the position of manager of the facility, which helped me finance four years of undergraduate education. I haven't been able to stand eggs since, but I adore chickens. When I saw that the NQOF challenge this year was Flying Geese, I knew I had to incorporate an avian species and a rooster came to mind immediately. I had already completed a rooster quilt but I wanted to improve upon the design. The tail feathers in my original quilt were pieced in chevrons, but I knew I wanted to incorporate the Flying Geese block in the tail on this quilt.

I sketched a line drawing of the rooster on 8½" x 11¼" paper, scanned it on a printer, and copied it to a transparency. I used an overhead projector to project and trace the image onto the dull side of a large sheet of freezer paper. The background vegetation, fence, and Flying Geese sun were subsequently drawn on the freezer paper as well. I added registration marks to facilitate reassembly of the units. The paper templates were cut apart and used to paper piece

the individual units. The rooster body and neck, row crops, grass, and fence were paper pieced as individual units.

I used Caryl Bryer-Fallert-Gentry's Applipiecing (curved piecing) method to join these units. Briefly, you apply liquid starch to the seam allowance with a paint brush and turn the fabric to the back of the freezer-paper template with a hot iron. Using a light box, align adjacent pieced templates using registration marks for reference. Temporarily join the aligned pieces with Scotch tape to facilitate stitching, then stitch together with invisible thread using a tiny zigzag stitch that just catches the edge of the folded top fabric. I use invisible thread on top and in the bobbin and drop the top tension.

I assembled the rooster (*sans* head and feet) and the vegetation and fence before I tackled drawing and piecing the background sun. I hand-drew the Flying Geese in the sun "rays" and spent several days piecing the sun. Then I auditioned the sun behind the rooster and was horrified to discover that I hated it.

While I have a large design wall, I often find it easier to audition backgrounds on my 8' x 8' table. The table is situated below a second-floor landing. I can run up the stairs, snap a picture, and repeat the process as many time as necessary while auditioning potential backgrounds. This process also provides me with a great workout!

Prior to piecing the sun, I had auditioned several batiks that gave the appearance of a rising sun. This is a good example of why one should listen to their gut instinct and first impression. The pieced sun was too "busy" and detracted from the rooster. So I opted to use the "sunrise" batik fabric. I loved this fabric and had purchased multiple yardage that I then hoarded while I waited for the perfect project. Once the background was added (again utilizing the Applipiecing method), I auditioned several fabrics for the head, comb, wattles, and feet/legs.

I traced the templates for these body parts onto freezer paper, ironed freezer templates onto the chosen fabric, and applied Mistyfuse® fusible web to the back of the fabric. The body parts were cut out, arranged appropriately, and fused to the background.

Quilting on the rooster, vegetation, and fence was done almost entirely free motion on a sit-down machine, as was the straight-line quilting in the background sky. I love variegated threads, and I found a perfect thread for the background. Unfortunately, it was an unfamiliar brand and I struggled to anchor the thread when starting and stopping. The thread ended up in the trash can and instead I used a variety of decorative polyester and rayon threads with invisible thread in the bobbin. I learned a valuable lesson: don't use an unknown variable in a special quilt.

The title was a piece of cake as I already had a rooster quilt of the same name. Roosters are the most reliable alarms! This is the second New Quilts from Old Favorites entry that I have finished with time to spare and I entered it in the Georgia National Fair. It received Best of Show honors.

Finalist

JANE ZILLMER

Mercer, Wisconsin

Meet Jane

Photo by Carla Fahden

As long as I can remember, I have been passionate about needle and thread. I took my first sewing class when I was nine years old and soon started stitching on my mother's old Singer® machine, making all my own clothes. In addition, I've enjoyed knitting, crocheting, embroidery, needlepoint—you name it. Hand-stitched wool appliqué is also a relaxing form of needle art for me.

My mother was a quilter; each of our beds had a handmade summer and winter quilt. Being frugal, she saved all fabric scraps. In my teens, I pulled out these scraps, organized them, and designed and created my very first quilt. It was machine pieced and later my mother hand quilted it for me. I still have that quilt. It reminds me of how far my quilts have evolved.

In 1989, I took my first actual quilting class and hand pieced a traditional sampler. I was immediately hooked and went on from there to make bed quilts, quilts to donate for raffles, quilts for gifts, and finally started making quilts just for me. After entering a small local quilt show and winning first place, I was spurred to continue entering my quilts in shows—regional, national, and international—and have won many awards.

I enjoy sharing my work with others and the fact that a quilt will be judged and seen by many people inspires me to do well and always improve my work.

I do consider my quilts to be more traditional than "art" per se, but I believe any creative work is art. Appliqué is my very favorite design element and machine appliqué is my favorite technique. My sewing studio overlooks Echo Lake and it is so peaceful to be completely absorbed in a project, working away there for hours.

My quilts and articles about them and my techniques have been featured in a number of publications. I have written a book, *Nature's Journey Appliqué*, published by the American Quilter's Society. It includes patterns and stories about seven of my quilts. Writing this book was a challenge in itself. I always dreamed of being an author and, well, I finally did it!

I'm often asked if I sell my quilts, and yes, recently I've sold a number of my earlier pieces. But I don't sell my show quilts; as I said, I make them for me. Many of them are very large, now starting to create a storage problem!

Quilting is what I am known for, it's me. I find time each day to do something quilt-related and there is always something to draw me in to my quilt world.

Inspiration and Design

Last March, on a brilliant, early spring day while out walking near my daughter and son-in-law's home in Orono, Minnesota, I spotted a flock of white geese flying overhead. I've seen many Canadian geese over the years, but never these.

When I returned to my home, my good friend Mark Brandt told me what I saw were migrating snow geese. I wanted to learn more about the snow goose and spoke in depth with Mark, who holds a degree in wildlife management and as a hobby has been bird watching for over 40 years. He has witnessed thousands of snow geese in North Dakota and Canada and says it is an impressive sight to see them en masse; their sound is deafening.

It is actually unusual for snow geese to be seen in the Midwest. Over the years they have moved west. The birds I saw are lesser snow geese, and Mark describes them as "kind of crazy birds." They were migrating, probably from Texas or Missouri, heading north into the tundra, Hudson Bay, or Baffin Island near the Arctic Ocean for the summer, which I find amazing. They are opportunists (most birds are)—they stay wherever there is food.

Their population exceeds five million. As grazers, they eat grain crops and pull up plants and eat them, root and all. In such huge broods, they are eating the tundra and destroying their nesting habitat.

As with most of my quilts, an inspiration comes to me at a special moment such as when I spotted the snow geese. I knew then that there was a quilt idea brewing, but not exactly what my design would be or when I'd get it started.

In 2015, I was a second-place winner in the New Quilts From an Old Favorite: Nine Patch challenge. It was such a great experience, I knew I would want to enter again. Then I discovered the 2017 challenge block would be Flying Geese. Perfect! Now was the time to design my quilt.

I thought it interesting that birds will migrate at night. How about MOONLIGHT MIGRATION as my theme and title?

I wanted to include as many geese as possible in my quilt depicting the sheer numbers of these snow geese. The background consists of pieced traditional Flying Geese blocks. I tend to like a Nine Patch layout. Nine moons were appliquéd over the background, then the geese migrating in the moonlight. The day I saw the geese flying overhead, I noted a single goose flying off by itself in a different direction. I depicted this in one of the moons.

Surrounding each moon is a stylized version of the traditional Flying Geese block, giving the image of flight or wings, with elongated and elegant blocks in the border to represent beautiful snow geese with their wings outstretched.

I love how I was able to tell the story of the snow goose in this quilt.

Technique

Quilt layout

For MOONLIGHT MIGRATION, as I usually do when designing a quilt, I started with the size quilt I wanted to make and then did some rough sketches of my background blocks. I turned to my trusty EQ7® quilt software program to help with fabric color choices and the quilt and border layout. I loved playing with the infinite color palette available here. Next, I printed background block cutting and piecing diagrams from EQ7.

While browsing Flying Geese block patterns in the EQ7 library, I found many interesting possibilities and surprised myself when sampling one of them in the border blocks. It gave a really dramatic effect. To get the proper size and exact templates I would need, I hand-drew the larger Flying Geese border blocks. For the corner border blocks, more Flying Geese were also found on EQ7 and the size was perfect; no need to redraw.

Fabric

I had fabric colors in mind—all of them already in my stash. I wanted the

background to be very dark to depict the night sky. The moon, wings, borders, and geese would all be done in neutral earthy tones of the snow goose.

Piecing

The background Flying Geese blocks showcase the only piecing involved in this entire quilt.

I machine appliquéd the moons to the pieced background blocks.

More design, drawing, and appliqué

This is when I decided to add the Flying Geese triangles surrounding each moon. The stylized diamond shape and free-flowing look reminded me of the geese in flight. Each of these pieces was machine appliquéd.

Then I needed to draw the actual goose. I studied many images of the snow goose, did a lot of sketching, and finally came up with a neat, graceful looking goose.

I appliquéd the geese flying across the sky in the moonlight. It took many attempts at pinning these geese on the background to get the effect I wanted.

On to the borders

The elongated Flying Geese blocks were machine appliquéd rather than pieced, then joined to form the borders.

Time to machine quilt

With all that is going on in this piece, choosing quilting designs became a challenge As I worked, I planned machine-quilting designs. I wanted the quilting to match the general feel of this quilt, not be linear or too graphic, not taking over the rest of the quilt, but complementing it. I sketched out quilting designs on paper.

Facing vs. binding

I chose wool batting, as I love its loft and ease of quilting. I basted my three layers using Sharon Schamber's hand-basting method (http://sharonschamber.com).

Rather than a traditional binding I chose instead a faced binding, giving the quilt a more artistic, finished look. I followed Cristy Fincher's technique as found in the July/August 2014 issue of *Machine Quilting Unlimited* (http://machinequilting.mqumag.com).

My machine-appliqué technique

Almost all of my quilts are composed primarily of raw-edge, machine-stitched appliqué. I do all of my drawing by hand with a lot of trial and error. Once perfected, I trace my motifs onto fusible web, HeatnBond® Lite being my favorite. To prevent a flat, stiff look, I cut a donut hole in the web before fusing it to fabric. Motifs are cut out and I start auditioning them on my background for color effect, placement, and size.

Once all is happy, motifs are fused to the background, usually in small sections.

Using a very narrow, short zigzag stich and my beloved #40 rayon or polyester threads, I machine appliqué all motifs in place. This is one of my favorite parts of the whole quiltmaking process.

The National Quilt Museum
Expanding the Vision, Advancing the Art

The National Quilt Museum brings the work of today's quilters to new audiences worldwide through exhibits, educational programs, and advocacy efforts.

Exhibits

The museum's in-facility and touring exhibits are annually viewed by over 115,000 quilt and art enthusiasts. The museum is a global destination welcoming visitors from all 50 U.S. states and over 40 foreign countries on a yearly basis. Visitors experience three galleries of extraordinary quilt and fiber art rotated seven to eight times per year, so there is always something new to see. The museum is among the highest rated tourism destinations on TripAdvisor, having won the TripAdvisor® Certificate of Excellence for the past four consecutive years.

The museum's touring exhibits can be seen at museums and galleries nationwide. Recent travelling exhibits have been seen in the Shafer Memorial Art Gallery, Great Bend, Kansas; the Harlingen Arts and Heritage Museum, Harlingen, Texas; and the Branigan Cultural Center, Las Cruces, New Mexico, among others.

Photo by Glenn Hall Photography

Education

Over 4,000 youth participate annually in museum educational programs such as: free student tours, summer quilt camp, Junior Quilters, Girl Scout programs, offsite visits to school classrooms, the Creative Arts Street Fair, involvement in community festivals, and hands-on activities that explore the many techniques found in quilt making.

The annual School Block Challenge contest is the most well-known program offered by the National Quilt Museum. It is open to students nationwide in grades K-12 and requires participants to create a quilt block using three challenge fabrics provided by Moda Fabrics. The 2017 contest and exhibit included 255 students from 16 different states and a total of 204 entries.

Museums, as a place of informal learning, can focus on the arts in a unique way to connect youth with subjects covered in traditional schooling: math, visual arts, history, science, nature, and life skills. Through this variety of programs, tours, and hands-on projects, The National Quilt Museum strives to teach the art of quilting to the next generation.

Advocacy

As part of the museum's mission to introduce the work of today's quilters to new audiences worldwide, museum staff work to educate the public through a variety of media and publicity efforts. Last year alone, over 300 publications wrote articles about the museum's work including Reuters news service, Yahoo.com, *USA Today,* and *Southern Living* magazine. Throughout the year the museum staff participates in talks and panel discussions at events worldwide. Recently, Museum Curator Judy Schwender spoke about the work of today's quilt community in Tokyo, Japan.

The National Quilt Museum is primarily funded through the generosity of the quilting community. If you are passionate about quilting, please go to www.quiltmuseum.org/support to see how you can get involved.

The National Quilt Museum is a 501(c)(3) nonprofit organization funded by quilters like you.